SOMETHING FOR THE WEEKEND

SOMETHING FOR THE WEEKEND

LIFE IN THE CHEMSEX UNDERWORLD

JAMES WHARTON

Biteback Publishing

First published in Great Britain in 2017 by
Biteback Publishing Ltd
Westminster Tower
3 Albert Embankment
London SE1 7SP
Copyright © James Wharton 2017

James Wharton has asserted his right under the Copyright, Designs and Patents Act 1988 to be identified as the author of this work.

Every reasonable effort has been made to trace copyright holders of material reproduced in this book, but if any have been inadvertently overlooked the publishers would be glad to hear from them.

ISBN 978-1-78590-229-1

10 9 8 7 6 5 4 3 2 1

A CIP catalogue record for this book is available from the British Library.

Set in Minion Pro

Printed and bound in Great Britain by
CPI Group (UK) Ltd, Croydon CR0 4YY

MIX
Paper from
responsible sources
FSC
www.fsc.org   FSC® C020471

To the gay men who are dying on G every twelve days in London, this one's for you.

CONTENTS

FOREWORD

We live in confusing and difficult times. We all have online profiles and spend our time posting photos of our perfect, flawless, photoshopped lives. We show our look, proclaim our uniqueness, all the while desperately wanting to belong. We have never been more connected with each other and with the world, yet we have never felt so lonely. This is the age of the individual, but still we feel pressure to conform, pressure for us all to be the same. The idea of a gay community should be a remedy, the very thing to pull us together, to help us belong, but still I find a bittersweet irony in the phrase 'the gay community'. Maybe we are a united community, once a year, when Pride comes around – and sometimes we're even united by Eurovision.

But otherwise divisiveness, judgement and abjection all too often underlie so much of what we do and say. And chemsex, a word I loathe and find gravid with prejudice, has become a nidus for so much of this division. This bloody, bold and agonisingly honest book shows this with uncompromising clarity.

It screams our pain and reveals our scorn. It will help many, horrify some and irritate a few. And that is exactly what a good book should do. It joins the ranks of Matthew Todd and Johann Hari as one of the defining social critiques of our time. Most importantly, it implores us as a society to change our views on drugs.

Drugs are not, or should not be, an issue of law but one of public health. However, thanks to the hysteria whipped up by tabloids, decriminalisation has become a dirty word – as dirty a word as 'chemsex' is to the *Daily Mail*. Prohibition is all that our legislators seem to know, despite overwhelming evidence against it. Harm to health caused by drug use is rising, and that harm is concentrated in vulnerable groups. The LGBTQ+ community is vulnerable; we are hurting from our mistreatment by society and the mistreatment we have suffered by our own hand (to quote *Hamlet*, 'the heartache, and the thousand natural shocks that/flesh is heir to'). Instead of wasting resources on punishment, we should focus on making society safe and on helping people to avoid, reduce or recover from drug-related harm.

As a young doctor, I worked for a time in Kenya; there I learned a wonderful Swahili word, *harambee*, meaning 'all pull together'. *Harambee* is a Kenyan tradition of community self-help – people fundraise for those in need and also initiate development activities to improve living conditions. Put simply, it is the act of kindness. We could benefit so much from such an attitude, from the same spirit of altruism. If ever there was a powerful cry for us to be better, wiser, more compassionate and eleemosynary, this book is it. Perhaps now fewer of us will feel the need to escape, to self-medicate, to isolate ourselves and ultimately end up feeling trapped. Help exists and everyone should be able to access it. The more we judge, the less we love. *Harambee.*

Dr Christian Jessen, July 2017

AUTHOR'S NOTE

Some names have been changed to protect the privacy of individuals.

1

SOMETHING FOR
THE WEEKEND

Friday afternoon, 4.30. The order has gone to my dealer: two bags of meph, 50ml of G. He replies via WhatsApp asking where he should drop the items off. 'Can you do London Bridge? I'm heading straight out.' He confirms and tells me he'll meet me there around six. 'Usual place.' Perfect. This is just one order of hundreds made in a similar fashion every Friday by gay men all over town to the many dealers covering the boroughs of the capital. It will cost me £70 and, once started, will leave me wanting neither food nor alcohol, due to the potency of mixing the ingredients together, meaning essentially, bar the Uber journeys from location to location I'll inevitably undertake in the hours and days following, £70 should be all the cost my weekend incurs. Until I run out of either drug and I can't stop myself from buying more, which is another inevitability.

Tonight's activity is a friend's house party celebrating his birthday in Dalston. Looking through the Facebook invite list, I can see the theme of the event is pretty much exclusively limited to drugs. Indeed, two fellow attendees have already messaged me asking if I can collect 'drinks' and 'mints' for them, the subtle terms adopted to describe the two aforementioned drugs. They are too late: my order has arrived and I don't intend to hassle Peter until I either run out of supplies myself and have returned to south London (he gets a little precious about travelling north of the river) or find myself accidentally hosting a gathering in my Balham flat, something that happens often. In this instance, Peter will be at mine swiftly, knowing the ten or so guys in my living room will likely all need supplying, a good earner for him. When this happens, Peter typically gives me my drugs for free, or at least provides me with extra at no additional cost.

I'm fairly late to the house party when I arrive; I always catch a friend for Friday drinks in Soho before starting my fun. He knows what I'm likely to be up to later, but doesn't judge. He'd prefer I didn't and offers an alternative plan, but I decline. As usual, I find it hard to give him my full concentration: all I can think about is seeing the boys and letting go of my cares over the course of a couple of lines and a large opening shot of the G.

By 1 a.m., and after my third shot of the juice, I finally feel on top of the world. I've barely touched my own supplies because there's so much going around the group. Crammed inside this apartment are about thirty guys, all in their late twenties or early thirties, all of whom are impressive in their own lives, and all of whom spend every weekend on another planet, carefree, just like me. Monday will come to each of us like a double-decker bus smashing through our lives, pushing us to reality. But that feels like a million miles away right now and nobody cares.

This is a chill-out. Everybody is doing the same drugs, or 'chems', as the using community refer to them. The word 'drugs' conjures up so much additional meaning; it's packed to the brim with judgement. When you think 'drugs', you think *Trainspotting*. 'Chems' is easier off the tongue and, although explicit, it doesn't feel quite as bad. At least to us.

Tops come off and we each appear to be wearing shorts. The host, Neil, will have handed out most pairs. 'Neil, have you got a pair of shorts I can borrow?' is a sentence I've heard said a dozen times, including by me. Everyone is euphoric. The effect of G, even though it's administered in the tiniest of doses – measured by a medical syringe to ensure precise levels and on a strict hourly basis – sends the user's mind whizzing within ten to fifteen minutes of swallowing. A friend once described the effect to me as being completely drunk, yet still being completely aware of one's surroundings. It is possible to push this too far, the dreaded 'going under' effect, but so far everybody's been OK. The music is turned up over the conversations, which span global politics, the latest Beyoncé track and anything else randomly entering the minds of us intelligent, but off our heads, savvy young adults. We are bobbing to the beats, sweat forming on our foreheads, and topping up the meph in our bloodstreams every ten minutes or so, either by snorting a line or, more likely, by bumping – placing some of the powder on the end of a key and sniffing the crushed-up crystals quickly up our nostrils.

Occasionally, two guys will disappear off together, perhaps to the toilet or to some other corner out of main view. G, or GBL to give it its proper title, is a sexual stimulant, and of course boys will be boys. But this is not a sex party, and nor will it turn into one. Horniness and fondling have to be done out of sight.

To an outsider, this entire situation would look alien. Nobody is drinking alcohol: people arrive clutching bottles of Pepsi, or another soft drink. We refer to these pop drinks as 'mixers', as they're only used to mix the minuscule measures of G we each pour ourselves, too bitter (frankly disgusting) to drink on its own.

And nothing else really happens. Everybody continues getting high, topping up their bodies with the drugs when the time is right. Nobody is being a dick, and nobody has, so far, taken too much. It begins to stale out a little around 2 a.m. and suddenly, it's time for a change of venue.

An army of Ubers are ordered. Somebody in the group has suggested we go on to theirs, another apartment, this time near Farringdon. The host sets off on the short car journey west with a couple of guys to set up; the rest of us follow in groups of four in our different cars. There's talk of ordering more chems, and other people, not yet seen this evening, will meet us there. The night, or morning as it now is, has renewed life, and as soon as we arrive we all take a large G to get us full-swing in the mood. This new gathering seems to be a little sexier and, indeed, the arrival of new people, who have each been at a club somewhere east, creates excitement. It feels OK to be a little more forward here: people are now wearing just their boxer shorts and the vibe has turned a little more sexual.

In one of the bedrooms, boys hang out on the bed. There's fumbling and kissing going on. But it's about as far as it's going at the moment. In the main living room and in the kitchen, the majority of the gang congregate. A plate with lines of varying sizes is passed around. Somebody announces they have some ketamine, and bodies start to manoeuvre to get a bump before it disappears. Ketamine is a drug that really lets its effects on the user be known. It can make everything around you appear different; the walls, the ground beneath you, the sky and even the stars appear as if they might all exist in a different reality. Some of us bump a small amount and about seven minutes later our minds are behaving in ways that we each find difficult to explain. Our grasp on reality, at least for a little while, has left us. Ketamine can be deadly when this happens.

There are some drop-offs from the party as the next couple of hours go by. These are either disciplined users, whom I admire, who have reached the time they set themselves to call it a day and go home, or guys who felt the vibe get a little too sexual for their liking and decided to break off to another, less sexually vibed, chill-out – or the opposite, some who have gone to a more full-on sex party, having found this to be a good starter. Perhaps we'll see them later? At about 10 a.m., the gathering in the flat in Farringdon starts to fizzle out. This causes me and a couple of others to panic: we still have supplies and don't want to call it a day. At this point, I usually either fall on my sword and pull the stragglers back to mine or go to my default setting: find a sex party. Fortunately, I know just where to find one.

Thirty minutes later, after a shot of G to send me on my way in the mood I want to remain in, I'm in an Uber heading to Stratford. Over in that part of town is a modern apartment which constantly has a gathering of guys within its walls. The owner of the property is himself a dealer, and can therefore provide his visitors with constant supplies, and himself with a lucrative flow of cash. I WhatsApp him from the car double-checking I can swing by; 'of course' comes his reply. I have pulled with me a friend, an older chap in his late forties, and an unknown guy I met at the last flat. The three of us will arrive at something completely different to what we've seen in the last twelve or so hours. This will be a group of somewhat strangers to each other, high on the drugs of their choice. Steven, whose flat it is, has everything one could wish for, and everyone there will be looking for sex. Some will be unattractive, some will be hot. None will have slept and all will be completely out of their minds. My two companions and I will do what we need to do to fit in within minutes of arriving, and after that pretty much anything goes. I have redonned my jeans, but the atmosphere at the next place will not require me to wear anything more than my underwear at most. We are going to a chemsex party.

I am, at this point, on to my second and final bag of meph. I have half a bottle of G – it was used by everyone at the last venue; it always seems to balance out, the sharing of supplies, and part of being allowed to turn up at Steven's Stratford pad is that we will spend money on his various stock. I agree to buy a bag and the boys say they will each do the same. We pool together what G we have left, and we discuss how long we'll each stay. All of it is irrelevant. We know the rules we make will be broken. I promised myself, just a day earlier, that I wouldn't buy any more drugs this weekend. And the last three occasions I was at Steven's, I stayed until the very early hours of Monday morning. I will likely be at this next place for thirty hours. Let's see.

We arrive and are not disappointed. It's a good-looking bunch of guys, all wearing practically nothing, and considering they've abused their bodies with everything from M and G to crystal meth over the course of the last day or so, some longer, they look in pretty good nick.

While stocking up, I also buy some Valium in preparation for when I do eventually have to come down, and two little blue pills: Viagra. The unfortunate, and quite ironic, side effect of all these chemicals is a penis that refuses to budge. Steven has been handing out the Vs in abundance for as long as boys have been high in his second-floor flat, two for a fiver.

Having scored my supplies and topped up on the hourly dot with G, I mingle with some of my newfound companions in the living room. Soon somebody's hand finds itself in my pants and I return the gesture. We are holding a conversation about each other's careers yet each fondling the other's chemically induced erection. There's a parliamentary researcher, a doctor; it feels completely OK to be here given how diverse the crowd is. Somebody gets up to cut some lines, and a plate is passed around the six of us leaning on various parts of the somewhat worn sofa. The signature sound of house music remains a constant, as does the need to consume chemicals in the regular fashion the body has become used to. Does anybody consider quitting and going home? No: there are drugs in abundance, hot guys and enough testosterone to sink a ship. The doorbell rings and more people arrive.

What's pulled each of us here? Addiction? A longing to be part of something? A need to escape life for a few days? Are there elements of self-hatred, or of not holding respect for one's self and dignity? Of course, it's all of these things, and there are many more reasons why this is as popular a weekend hobby as visiting art galleries in London. As wacky and dangerous as this weekly dive into craziness is, I never stop to pull my head away from the plate that's passed before me. We are all in this together. We know it's fucking up our lives, and we know it will come to an end one way or the other. It has to, right?

But hey, giving up is not on my mind right now. And fuck it, I feel on top of the world. I have hot guys never before introduced to me pulling at my underwear, dragging me off to the bathroom, sharing their chems with me. I feel popular, an ecstasy in itself: my body is being validated and people like me.

This is of course wholly the effect of the drugs on my mind. I look terrible, I can't think straight and I smell a bit. I haven't eaten anything, I look gaunt, and although I'm only midway through this debauchery, I've already had sexual contact with at least ten different guys. I'm a fucking mess.

A day later, having spent another £100 on supplies, I am eventually done. I order an Uber and I return to my flat ten miles away in south London. I am exhausted, yet not tired. I am hungry, but without an appetite. My mind is full of faces and encounters of the past two days, but I am unfulfilled. I need to shower, to brush my teeth, to get something, anything, into my stomach. But I don't. I walk through the door, I glance at the many messages on Facebook from friends and family worried about why I've been so silent all weekend, again, and I collapse onto my bed. I drop the Valium and become numb. I close my eyes and, in an instant, it's time to go to work. That double-decker bus of a Monday morning, and reality, has arrived.

I will feel like shit until about lunchtime on Wednesday, and then I'll start to think about the weekend again. It's a cycle I can't stop.

2

STATE OF THE NATION

In 2017, as an entire country – regardless of sexuality – it is right that we mark the fiftieth anniversary of the Sexual Offences Act, an Act that decriminalised sex in private between men over the age of twenty-one in England and Wales.

Legislatively speaking, it was a start. In the years that followed, many battles would be fought and eventually won: levelling the age of consent; achieving equality across the border in Scotland; removal of the dreadful Section 28, which instructed councils not to 'intentionally promote homosexuality or publish material with the intention of promoting homosexuality' in schools and workplaces. There are many other victories to celebrate, too: civil partnerships, same-sex marriage, the Equality Act, the pardon afforded all those like gay hero Alan Turing, who were convicted for simply being themselves before the introduction of this historic Act. In fact, since 27 July 1967, when the Sexual Offences Act was enforced, we gay members of Great Britain have been on an upward trajectory, surviving Tory attempts in the 1980s and 1990s to suppress us, to stop us becoming what we are today: equal.

But that's just the law. Every step forward on paper has had to be matched by a societal acceptance and embracing of this steady dawning of gay equality, and that hasn't always been straight-forward. Whereas the law has generally (and I say generally) moved to protect LGBT people, some parts of the country, and people, have been slow to embrace it and in many cases have actively fought against it: the Church, Thatcherism and Northern Ireland's continued refusal to grant equal marriages are just a few examples I can cite. And who can forget the candlelit vigil that was held in 1990, commemorating the five gay men who were murdered within months of each other on the streets of London.

In an interview for *Winq* magazine in 2015, Sarah Kate Ellis, CEO of the US-based GLAAD (Gay & Lesbian Alliance Against Defamation), told me that 'as policy moves forward, culture starts to lag behind' – an expression that I think aptly describes the situation for LGBT people in this country, although Sarah was actually talking about the atmosphere at the time in the United States. Legislation can never progress quickly enough when talking about human rights, of course, but perhaps the problem we face in the UK is that the legislation did advance, but at a speed that not everyone could keep up with. Sadly, a unified position on LGBT equality has never existed.

Nowhere is this better depicted than in the 2014 film *Pride*, in which a group of 1980s London-based gay men and women rally together to raise funds for striking miners in Wales. When the metropolitan gays arrive at the small mining community to hand over the money, there is hostility towards the 'queer' and 'perverted' out-of-towners. To some, the hostility might have merely seemed a glimpse into a bygone era, a time that has been consigned to the history books. But as someone who grew up in a similarly small Welsh community in the late 1990s and early 2000s, with a local economy that was faltering compared to that of our flourishing cosmopolitan cousins across the English border, what I saw in the film was typical of the ignorance that went hand in hand with a rural community upbringing. *Pride* presents us with men and women who have chosen to settle in London despite not hailing from the capital. In 1984, London was their haven; they followed the bright lights to the city where they could be, in spite of Thatcherism and the unfolding AIDS crisis, to an extent, themselves – something that was impossible at home. Let's remember that.

Some parts of the UK have been more forward-thinking and quicker off the mark as the ascent to equality has taken flight. There are places – London, Manchester and Brighton – that have been more accommodating and culturally sympathetic towards gay people during the gruelling journey to reach where we are today, and as a result these places have become the main UK hubs for the LGBT community. Most of us packed up our lives and headed to one of these areas because where we came from wasn't the right place for the people we were. We were, in effect, outsiders.

When I first arrived in London, in 2004, I found it surprisingly easy to become part of the gay community and for the first time in my young life I felt I was part of something. Friends were made, relationships forged, fun had. But all around me were people and places that had been scarred of our journey to equality. It has not been plain sailing; there have been many obstacles we have had to navigate along the way – let's not forget the disgusting bombing of the Admiral Duncan pub on Old Compton Street in 1999. I think of that terrible attack every time I enter or walk past the place.

Encountering this inequality, either at first hand or via someone else's story, has left us to some extent angry. A mere mention of how the government made it illegal to talk about homosexuality in schools, or how the Vatican encouraged people not to use condoms because it 'aided the spread of HIV', helps people get the message: we're pissed off.

If we look at the LGBT community today, moving beyond the fifty-year anniversary of decriminalisation, what we see is a huge human picture composed of many different identities. Even the term LGBT, which stands for lesbian, gay, bisexual and transgender, is criticised by some as being too narrow-minded. Some might ask, and rightly so, about the inclusion of queer people, or of unisexuals, pansexuals and, of course, asexuals. Even just honing in on one area, gay men for example, we are all incredibly different. Take me, for instance. I've been a fresh-faced young man on the scene, trying to cram everything and everybody into my nights out; a married twenty-something in a committed relationship; a country boy who likes walks on a Sunday with his dog; an inner-city single; a party boy; a scene queen and a chemsex addict, all by the age of thirty. Life for all of us in our so-called community is different. When you look at things in this way, it's perhaps easier to understand why some people refuse to label themselves as anything at all, something which is becoming more common among millennials. Equality has progressed, but it hasn't accounted for individualism; instead it's grouped us all together as 'one', when we are actually anything but. We simply are not as similar as we are told to believe.

Of course, everything didn't just become OK overnight back in 1967. But save the occasional snag, homosexual males progressed through the '70s and into the early '80s in what must have felt like an alien world compared to the days when you could be chemically castrated for being gay. Bigotry was still common, and times remained tough for those who were discovered to be gay, or who were brave enough to be out and proud, but in places like London, men could unite and live in relative safety. Again, the difference between the urban city and rural town was pronounced.

And then, just as things were going well, the world changed.

It's impossible to summarise in just a few words the impact that AIDS has had on all of us, regardless of whether you've lived through its terrible epidemic or you're a twenty-something who has never witnessed at first hand somebody's final days in an AIDS ward. You may have only seen images on the internet, or you might have buried a lover, but whether you lived through it or not the emotional impact of knowing that people just like you died through no fault of their own is tremendous. And if you did live through it, then those memories are etched into your mind for ever.

For many young gay men today, the 1980s AIDS crisis evokes images of fear. This is good if it encourages people to educate themselves about practising safe sex. But it is terrible if it pushes a person towards stigmatised ignorance. *Are you clean?* Three words brimming with stigma and often uttered by people enquiring about another person's medical status. What does this question infer at its core? And today, hiding behind the cloaks of anonymity that instant messaging apps and social media provide us with, people can verbalise their fear in the most sickening of ways, with a complete disregard for the feelings of fellow human beings. This isn't limited to HIV shaming, but also to ethnicity, body shape and size: for a so-called community, we do a very good job of ostracising people.

Technology has radically changed the ways we communicate with each other. In fact, for gay people globally, it's hard to imagine anything as game-changing as the invention of social apps that allow you to speak privately to like-minded people. Apps like Grindr and Hornet have allowed gay people in Moscow, who are living in fear, to spread messages of support and to unite; they let people who are not yet ready to fully come out to decide, at their own pace, how involved with the gay community they want to be. But because they are so easy to access, sometimes these apps are also used by people whose intentions are not always good, and things can end tragically. The surge in popularity of social apps, occasionally called 'sex apps', sometimes labelled 'hook-up apps', has revolutionised the ways in which two or more gay men can arrange to meet; it's hugely different today from how your average John and Dave would have met and fell in love fifty years ago, just as the law changed allowing them to be together.

But hang on, I hear you say, what does any of this have to do with drugs, and more specifically chemsex? Well, I'm afraid it all matters. Everything that's gone before us matters, and to try to guess why so many gay people, in London and beyond, are deciding to embrace this culture, we need to take stock of all the stuff that makes us 'us': concerns about AIDS, instances of slut-shaming, issues concerning Section 28 and so much more. And as we examine this world of drug use and sexual pleasure, we'll pause to examine the often complex motivating factors that compel people to do what they do, as well as asking some-times uncomfortable questions about who and what we are as a so-called 'community'. Is it a case of us all being fucked off with our lives? It's normal to hear people say 'chems help me escape the mundane realities of life' and 'when I'm high, all my worries just slip away'. Is it simply a case of people wanting to push the 'fuck it' button on a Friday night and have a good time? Before we attempt to answer these questions, we need to get an idea of how popular drugs are among gay people. Only then can we look further and explore motivations, routes in and, where necessary, routes out of the modern phenomenon that is chemsex.

According to a 2009 study conducted by the LGBT Foun-dation (the LGBT Foundation was then known as LGF), gay men living in the UK were seven times more likely to abuse drugs and alcohol than the rest of the population. These figures are incredible, and there are other surveys, reports and research that suggest that the number of drug users among the gay com-munity is higher than in any other social group. Simply put, if you are gay, you are more likely to take drugs.

In 2014, for the first time in many years, crime statistics for drug-related offences in England and Wales were analysed by sexual orientation. Incredibly, they showed that gay and bisexual men were three times more likely to use drugs than their heterosexual counterparts. The findings indicated an even greater gap between lesbian and bisexual women and straight women: LGBT women were almost four times more likely to be using drugs in the same year. Even at a quick glance these figures showed there was something within the LGBT community that made us all, regardless of gender, more likely to access illegal drugs. This might make uncomfortable reading for some, and of course the majority of LGBT people in the UK do not 'abuse' drugs, but it is impossible to look the other way and pretend there isn't a sizeable group of us who do.

Writing for PinkNews following the release of these stats, Monty Moncrieff, CEO of London Friend, a charity that specialises in helping LGBT people with drug-addiction issues, commented that there were also:

Large differences in 'club' drugs such as ecstasy (almost five times higher in LGBT people) and ketamine (seven-and-a-half times more common) ... One of the more noticeable discrepancies is the use of methamphetamine, or crystal meth. Globally the drug has been cited by the United Nations as the number one problem substance, and has caused devastation among users in many countries. In the UK, use is still very low, although we see here that it's almost all among gay and bi men.

Just read that last bit again: crystal meth in the UK is almost exclusively being used by gay and bi men. The article practically tells you that crystal meth in the UK is a gay drug. Moncrieff further stressed this point elsewhere in his article, revealing that 51 per cent of service users at Antidote (London Friend's drug counselling service) named crystal meth as their drug of choice. Missing from the released crime statistics were specific figures on the usage of GBL, a drug central to the sex-drug culture. But in his 2014 article, Monty Moncrieff pointed out that abuse of GBL among gay men had risen to alarmingly high levels, adding that in the 'last year 46 per cent of Antidote clients seeking drug treatment was for GHB/GBL'. Gay Men Fighting AIDS, commonly known as GMFA, is an important and non-judgemental charity which provides help and advice on HIV, sex, drugs and alcohol. It says the likelihood of gay men using drugs is now even higher than the figures in the 2014 Crime Survey for England and Wales suggest.

The Gay Men's Sex Survey 2014, commissioned by the Terrence Higgins Trust, asked respondents if they had 'EVER taken recreational or illicit drugs' – and if so, which ones and how recently? The results were staggering: over half of us said we'd tried illegal substances (52 per cent), with cannabis leading the way (48.6 per cent), followed by ecstasy (32.6 per cent) and cocaine just behind (32.2 per cent). But what was perhaps most interesting were the responses to how recently people had taken drugs: over 15 per cent of us had used ecstasy (or, as we will see in the next chapter, MDMA) in the year prior to the survey and 17 per cent had used cocaine. But all of this, so far, still doesn't get down to the nitty-gritty of chemsex. So let's look at what we know about chemsex, in terms of popularity and scale.

The 2014 Chemsex Study defines chemsex as 'sex between men that occurs under the influence of drugs taken immediately preceding and/or during the sexual session'. The study is considered the most authoritative piece of work on the subject and was commissioned by the London boroughs of Lambeth, Southwark and Lewisham – the three most densely populated areas with adult gay men in England. Within these three areas, the report's introduction tells us, there are also a high number of off-scene commercial gay bars and venues. In Vauxhall there is the major 'heavy' gay clubbing scene, in Southwark there's XXL, with its large 'sex-on-premises' or darkroom space, and, although shrinking in numbers since the report was commissioned, many saunas.

As part of the study, MSM (men who have sex with men) sex and drug habits from across the three boroughs were explored and the results compared against those of the wider London area, and then of England as a whole. The study found that Lambeth, Southwark and Lewisham were 'population centres for gay men, people living with HIV and recreational drug use', and further revealed that drug use among gay men was 'higher here than in any other region of England'. The report indicated that 'poly drug use' was the norm among the gay using community, although the use of more traditional drugs like LSD and speed had declined. The number of people using crystal meth, GBL and mephedrone had increased, with meph having surged in popularity extremely quickly. The study also found that cigarettes and booze were more popular among the under-30s, Viagra and poppers more fashionable with the over-40s and illicit drugs used mainly by those in their 30s. Interestingly, it stated that 'illicit drug use, injecting and concern about drug use [were] all significantly more common among men diagnosed with HIV'.

As part of the study's 'qualitative phase', a number of men who had used drugs in a sexual setting within the previous twelve months answered questions about their own chemsex habits. The study found that among this group 'many participants felt that mephedrone was so widely used on the commercial gay scene that it was inescapable', and where GBL was concerned, 'it was considered very cheap and widely available and many men reported that it relaxed them, increased their confidence and made them "horny"'. It's these key qualities that have made GBL and mephedrone so damn popular.

The study remains extremely relevant and, despite being published in 2014, it's still used to measure where we are as a community and to put our relationships with drugs in a sexual context. But in order to get some figures that were 'hot off the press', I spoke to David Stuart, the substance and misuse lead at the 56 Dean Street sexual health clinic. He told me that:

Approximately 3,000 gay men accessing 56 Dean Street's services each month are using chems. The majority of these are seeking help with the consequences of chems – like accessing PEP, being treated for STIs and getting HIV tests – but not actively seeking support for their chem use. Just an average of 100 gay men per month actively seek support from our chemsex support service.

It's a fascinating funnel: 3,000 go into the machine and 100 opt for support. But how many get fixed? There are those who openly talk about their drug use when accessing sexual health services at Dean Street, and others who go a step further and seek support for their drug habit. A mere three in every 100 of those who use the drugs most associated with chemsex feel they have a problem. It's quite a statistic.

I can recall a number of occasions over the years when I have visited Dean Street and been asked candidly whether I use chems. Had someone asked me this question when I was younger, I would have recoiled and shaken my head insistently. Back then I hadn't come across this part of our culture, and so by default I disliked it. A couple of years ago, after becoming a little more educated on drugs and their place in our culture, I found myself back at 56 Dean Street, only this time, when asked the same questions, I found myself replying yes to one or two of them. The nurse didn't so much as bat an eyelid; it was all very business-like. Obviously, it's imperative to have an understanding of a person's sexual behaviour when determining if and what treatment might be required, and the easiest way to gain an idea of someone's sexual behaviour is to ask direct and often probing questions about their personal life. But I couldn't help feeling that it was easier to ask these questions in London than it would have been anywhere else.

David's figures also suggest that roughly 97 per cent of those who admit to using drugs every month are happy to continue doing so without seeking any support for their use. Are we all happily snorting away without a care in the world? The statistics might suggest so.

Sex while under the influence of drugs is certainly not a new concept. Tales of people hanging out in opium dens, getting high and having sex are well documented; and, of course, there's the example of the Swinging '60s, when sex, drugs and rock 'n' roll were the craze for so many people. The fascination with using drugs to reduce inhibitions and achieve a euphoric state that can enhance sexual desire dates back centuries and has occurred frequently throughout history. But since the turn of the millennium, something has fuelled a sudden surge in drug use among gay men of all ages, who are united in the sexual gratification that drugs afford them. Although drug use among the gay community isn't new, never has it been so widespread. And I want to know why. Did we suddenly wake up one morning and decide to give chemsex a go? No, of course not. So when did this boom happen, and what brought it on?

'The introduction of mephedrone took chemsex into the big time; it brought it to a whole new city,' David Stuart tells me.

Before mephedrone came along, we used to just smoke crystal meth. A flight attendant used to fly it in from either San Francisco or Cape Town or somewhere, and about forty of us would smoke it in a sauna. That was chemsex among gay men in London in the early noughties. It was so few people compared to today.

By 'introduction', David is referring to the rediscovery of mephedrone in 2003. It was invented, or synthesised, in 1929 but remained largely unknown until 2003, when it was rediscovered – and was also legal to possess. In just a couple of years mephedrone became available to buy online, and shortly after that you could also find it on the high street. The original legal high, due to its cocaine- and MDMA-like qualities, mephedrone became hugely popular among university students around the world, but particularly in the UK. Because of the ease with which it could be sourced, and also its affordability, mephedrone established itself on the otherwise expensive London gay scene. Everyone went mad for it. This is reflected in the 2014 Chemsex Study, which indicates that the use of speed and LSD fell, coinciding with the rise in the popularity of mephedrone.

Mephedrone is one of the three components of what is often, and it must be said sometimes romantically, referred to as the 'unholy trinity' of chemsex drugs. The other two are G and Tina. But what exactly are they? What keeps users texting dealers throughout the weekend, topping up their supplies and their bloodstreams? What are these drugs?

3

TINA, MANDY, MOLLY AND THE GANG

Nice, aren't they, the nicknames we give to our drugs? The girls mentioned above are not people, but they're popular – very popular.

We use nicknames because they make the whole thing that little bit more palatable. Nobody wants to hear words like 'crystal' and 'meth' muttered on the Tube or in the street. A word like 'Tina' humanises the situation; it just feels so much better. Of course, there's the whole discretion thing, too: 'Hi mate, can you pop over? Bring Tina with you. Thanks.' You'd be none the wiser if you heard someone uttering those words into his phone while on the number 7 bus. That's a typical order for a dealer, asking him to bring crystal meth, the drug made more famous in this country thanks to the hit TV show *Breaking Bad*, an export from the USA.

Crystal meth is as good a place to start as any, but it's rarely the only substance a person will use. We'll now look at the most commonly used drugs on the London chemsex scene.

CRYSTAL METH

Tina, Meth, Ice, Glass, Crank

Its official name is methamphetamine and it's a Class A drug. In terms of people using the substance, it generally comes later on in the journey – for a lot of users it is a drug they graduate to. Those who do use it sometimes turn to it to help them get through the day. After a long weekend of partying, Monday morning suddenly hits you like a ton of bricks, and I really can't emphasise enough just how awful that feeling really is. People struggling to merely exist on a Monday smoke Tina because they feel it's the only way to overcome the dreaded comedown from all the other drugs they've taken. But, of course, there's bound to be a comedown from Tina too and that's considered the worst comedown of all. Its immediate effects include feeling exhilarated, very 'up' and awake, and, like a couple of the other chems that we'll look at in this chapter, it's a libido-enhancing drug, and therefore popular on the chemsex scene. As is the case with crack cocaine, most of the time Tina is smoked through a glass pipe. But it can also be *slammed*, the word that is used in the culture instead of 'injected'. As well as the come-down from hell, other negative effects include feeling agitated, paranoid, aggressive and confused. It is possible to overdose on Tina, with the severest reactions resulting in a coma or even death, although these are rare. Because the preferred method for some is to inject the drug, there is a greater risk of catching HIV, due to needle sharing. One other common effect is the haggard, malnourished look that heavy users can develop. In a nutshell, Tina makes you look like shit.

Tina is also bloody expensive, and a real drain on your finances because it's so addictive. A gram will set you back about £100, and might last a steady user a couple of days if they're smoking it alone. But if that gram is shared at a party by a few people, then it will very probably have vanished within twelve to twenty-four hours. Tina comes in tiny crystal-like rocks that vaporise when heated up. It is then inhaled through a pipe, or the rocks are placed in warm water and then slammed. The effects are pretty much instantaneous when the latter method is used.

The drug is hugely popular in the United States, hence *Breaking Bad*, which no doubt acted as a marketing campaign of sorts. Other major international hotspots include Australia, where the number of people regularly using it has tripled over the past five years, according to National Drug and Alcohol Research Centre estimates. During the same period in the UK, according to the *Metro* newspaper, crystal meth has become the 'new "trendy" drug in Britain' and arrests involving the drug have increased by 500 per cent. The newspaper also said the drug was best known for 'destroying lives, and turning its users into desperate, emaciated criminals'. However, we could accuse the *Metro* of sensationalising an issue and judging a group of vulnerable people all at once. Earlier, we learned that here in the UK, crystal meth is almost exclusively used by people who identify as gay or bisexual.

MEPHEDRONE

M, Meph, Meow Meow, M-Cat

Before I was introduced to M, which, depending on what part of the country you hail from, might also be referred to as M-Cat or meow meow, the only drug that I had ever really tried was cocaine, and so coke was the only thing that I could reasonably compare M to. After trying M, and quite liking it, I stopped occasionally taking coke and found myself doing meph more and more often, and at my peak I would do it every weekend and sometimes even in the week. In terms of addictiveness, I think it's important to say that, although I know people who have become hooked on cocaine, I was never one of them: I could always take it or leave it. What I found within hours of trying mephedrone, though, was that I wanted more and more... and then more. Eventually, I wouldn't even consider going out and seeing people without a supply of mephedrone in my pocket.

Mephedrone was the turning point for me: I was becoming more than just your typical, casual user, who might do a little coke at the weekend. Meph is a real gateway drug. When my addiction was at its worst, I would buy a number of grams on a Friday and stay awake for seventy-two hours, snorting a line every fifteen minutes to keep myself going. It's a stimulant, and when taken in conjunction with other drugs, can be depended upon to keep a user high, incredibly awake and feeling euphoric. Another side effect is that it makes you feel affectionate towards the people around you, and for this reason, it is extremely popular on the chemsex scene.

Until 2010, this drug was legal. It made a lot of headlines towards the end of the 'legal high' period. Meow meow will be familiar to many for outraging the middle classes when the substance was made available on their high streets, allowing local kids to get freely off their tits at the weekends. But today it's made quite the jump, and it is now a Class B drug. Officially, and by that I mean according to some of the leading drug information services out there, the effects of the substance last for about an hour, and the high provided by the drug is not too dissimilar to the highs that are offered by cocaine and ecstasy. But the stuff that's now being pushed around the scene in London is generally of poor quality; a line's desired effect doesn't last much longer than fifteen minutes at best. In fact, it's common to hear a long-term user say with annoyance: 'Back in the day, when meph was good...' As it has grown more popular, meph has become less potent. Something else to consider is affordability. Meph is usually available at £20 a gram, and because of this people buy lots of it, use lots of it and become addicted.

The *Daily Mirror* reported in 2015 that mephedrone's effects on heavy users include 'extreme weight loss, sudden crying and "a smell of cat wee"', which is a pretty damn accurate summary. On a comedown, which can be as awful as battling through a day without sleep, the potent smell of cat piss and sweat lingers. If someone has had a heavy weekend of mephedrone-fuelled fun, the smell oozing out of their pores is noticeable. As the *Mirror* points out, meph also affects your weight; it was my 'gauntness', as Mum put it, that set alarm bells ringing for her and this, in turn, ultimately became a turning point for me.

However, one thing the *Mirror* article doesn't mention – nor many drug help sites either – is the effect the drug has on one's intelligence. I firmly believe that the longer a person does meph, the less intelligent they become. I experienced this at first hand. I have always been a fairly clear-thinking kind of guy: I'm creative and filled to the brim with information that's both useful and useless. But about six months into regularly using mephedrone, I noticed that I just wasn't as sharp as I used to be. Things that had once been obvious to me were no longer so obvious, and my memory is now nothing like it used to be either. Mephedrone has really affected my brain. Even navigating my hands around a keyboard requires a lot more concentration than it did before. This type of side effect is referenced hardly anywhere, but from discussions with other people and from my own personal knowledge (albeit damaged), I think this is a major side effect that should be talked about more.

And lastly, like crystal meth, this drug is often slammed.

GBL/GHB

G, Gina, Liquid Ecstasy

GHB and GBL are different drugs, but almost all G found on the London scene is GBL. From here on, we'll refer to the substance as either G or GBL. GBL is converted into GHB after it is consumed.

G is the final member of the 'unholy trinity' of chemsex

drugs. Contrary to popular belief, it's also the most addictive. As a substance, G is actually more addictive than heroin and can require medically supervised withdrawal from dependency. It's the major player on London's gay drugs scene, and addiction has become an issue for so many people that in 2016 it was announced that a medical trial would commence involving 230 addicts. It's hoped that this trial will pave the way to get users off the drug and steer them away from the lifestyle that it is so intrinsically associated with. I firmly believe that just one 'shot' of this chemical is enough to get a user hooked.

G makes you more relaxed. It gives you confidence, gets you horny as hell and makes your head spin – all at the same time. But all this comes with a huge risk: just a drop – literally a millilitre – too much of G, and you are dicing with death. No scaremongering here, it's simply a fact. If you take even just the tiniest amount too much, or you forget how long it has been since you last drank some, then you will 'go under' – and the consequences of this can too often prove fatal.

It's the positive effects of G that make it so central to the gay chemsex scene: the buzz you feel when your mind is spinning; how it stimulates you sexually, lowering your inhibitions and making you feel fantastic. G is electrifying when you take it with mephedrone and Tina while having sex. But, again, there are risks.

In 2015, super-gonorrhoea emerged as a new infection that doctors were finding increasingly difficult to treat. *The*

Guardian reported that: 'The strain is highly resistant to the antibiotic Azithromycin, which means medics are relying on a second drug, Ceftriaxone, to treat it. But there are no other effective drugs to tackle the strain, raising the prospect of it becoming untreatable if it builds further resistance.'

Of course, this infection is not limited to gay men. And it wasn't until the issue began to affect straight people that the press really started to report on it. Sexual health clinics in London had been dealing with gay men affected by super-gonorrhoea for some time before *The Guardian* raised the subject. When high on G, sometimes people's inhibitions are lowered to such a degree that they might take risks they usually would avoid, which can include having sex without a condom. On World AIDS Day in 2016, Public Health England (PHE) announced that the number of gay men living with HIV in London had risen from one in eight in 2014 to one in seven in 2016. People are most likely to contract the disease from being intimate with someone who has HIV but is not yet undergoing treatment.

My own experience of the dark world of chemsex is that while sometimes people are aware enough to use condoms, many people often do not – perhaps by choice; perhaps because their inhibitions have been lowered so much that they feel it's fine not to use one. In some cases, people are so fucked up that they have no idea if a condom is being worn or not. Whatever the reason, not using a condom is common in the chemsex world. And perhaps this worry prompted NHS England to issue a public health warning about the dangers of chemsex:

The growth in use of illegal psychoactive substances during sex could pose an increasing risk to public health, experts say.

The popularity of 'chemsex' – mostly but not exclusively among gay men – is leading some sexual health services to set up special clinics to treat the consequences of drugs such as GBL and crystal meth.

Users are turning to such sources to lower inhibitions and increase pleasure, according to an editorial in the BMJ [*British Medical Journal*] by experts in sexual health and drug misuse.

G can be purchased for industrial use. It is also used occasionally in healthcare, due to its anaesthetic properties. But possessing and supplying the substance for consumption, away from these controlled environments, is illegal. As G is a Class C drug, you risk spending up to two years in jail if you are found in possession of it or fourteen years if you are caught dealing. It's a clear liquid, so it's easy to fill an empty water bottle and walk around without anybody knowing what's in it, but again, it could be deadly if someone were to pick the bottle up and take a gulp.

In terms of price, G is very cheap – about £1 per millilitre. When you consider the cost of a night out in a bar in London, how far would £50 get you? Probably not very. It's perhaps even easier to understand the appeal of the drug when you factor this next element into the cost equation: users of G won't drink alcohol when they're on it, as it's incredibly dangerous to mix G with booze. You can spend £50 at the start of a weekend on G and experience a level of intoxication five times that of alcohol. And you will have enough of the drug to last you for days.

COCAINE
Coke, Crack, Charlie, C

Coke is like a rat in London; you're never too far away from it. On the streets of Soho, you can score a gram of Charlie, of varying quality, within seconds. We are drowning in the stuff. Incredible really, when you consider that it is a Class A drug and that being found in possession of it can land you in prison for seven years. Dealing in coke can result in a life sentence. Yet I merely need to open my office window and shout down the street, and I'm in business (OK, not literally, but you get the point).

The cost of a gram depends on quality. If you want to spend only £60, then expect to be somewhat disappointed. If you are prepared to splash out on the 'good stuff', this will set you back over £100. However, there's a lot of poor-quality coke doing the rounds these days and you would be a fool to buy from someone you didn't already know.

Most commonly, people snort cocaine using a rolled-up banknote, after the coke has first been crushed into a powder. Sometimes people will smoke rocks of the stuff, which is referred to as crack cocaine. Although it makes occasional appearances on the chemsex scene, cocaine is not overly popular because it is so expensive: a weekend bender on coke could set you back £500, or possibly even more. Meph is much cheaper. And although not quite as good as coke, meph can still provide much the same sort of kick, so it is therefore more likely to be the drug of choice for many people.

Cocaine comes with some serious health risks – the major one being heart failure. The whole purpose of the drug is to raise alertness, energy levels and your heartbeat: coke gets you high physically. People with underlying, sometimes undiagnosed, health problems put themselves in significant danger when taking cocaine. Like all drugs, it's addictive. Because of how expensive it is, it can also easily bleed you dry, and this can have quite devastating knock-on effects on the rest of your life. Something else worthy of mentioning, and which people often snigger at, is the damage coke can do to cartilage in your nose that separates the nostrils. There is, of course, the famous Danniella Westbrook story about how the ex-*EastEnders* actress literally snorted away the inside of her nose, and people have turned the story into a bit of a joke. But every drugs advice service out there will warn you about this real possibility.

In December 2016, *The Guardian* reported that Londoners snort more cocaine during the working week than people in any other European city. Only one location outdid the UK capital at the weekend: Antwerp. To conduct the survey, sewage from fifty European cities across eighteen countries was analysed to measure the concentrated levels of cocaine found in the waste. I wasn't over-exaggerating when I told you about its popularity.

Cocaine was once available to purchase over the counter in Harrods, and despite it no longer being legal, a seemingly endless supply enters the UK every day; it's impossible to see the popularity of this drug dipping anytime soon. But while cheaper mephedrone remains the drug of choice, cocaine is unlikely to boom in the chemsex world.

MDMA (METHYLENEDIOXYMETHAMPHETAMINE)
Molly, Mandy, Ecstasy

Nobody says 'E' any more: it's all MDMA this, MDMA that. Madonna released an album in 2014 called *MDNA*, cheekily playing on the name of this popular substance. As far as marketing goes, they say it's all about knowing your audience.

MDMA is less a sex drug and more a party drug, but it does frequently feature on London's chemsex scene. People don't take ecstasy tablets any more; it's crushed into a powder and snorted instead, or dabbed on gums. MDMA is the chemical name for ecstasy, but it is now also the name that is almost exclusively used when referring to the drug.

It's a stalwart of London nightlife. Clubbers have been using MDMA for twenty years to help them dance the night away and rave; its ability to energise has made it popular on the all-nighter scene. I've had conversations with friends, now in their fifties, who still reminisce about taking MDMA when they were twenty-five. It's stood the test of time.

Another important thing to point out is that, like cocaine,

MDMA is a Class A drug. As well as giving users a burst of energy, it allows them to feel 'in tune' with their peers and their surroundings. It encourages you to be more affectionate, which perhaps justifies its place on the chemsex scene, even if only as a secondary drug. It also makes you chatty (very chatty). There's a famous scene in the cult 1999 coming-of-age film about drugs and club culture, *Human Traffic*, that portrays this well. But despite the health risks associated with the drug, MDMA may soon be used as a medical treatment. In the United States, in 2016, MDMA was approved by the Food and Drug Administration for medical testing, with the intention of using it as a treatment for post-traumatic stress disorder (PTSD), the condition most commonly associated with armed conflict. This substance could, very possibly, be legally prescribed in the not too distant future to improve mental health stateside, and further afield. Currently, MDMA costs about £40 per gram in London.

So there you have it. Suddenly, when you understand more about some of the consequences of taking these drugs, those pet names referenced at the beginning of this chapter appear a little more sinister. But all these various substances, the kicks they provide and the repercussions they carry, lead us back to one person: the drug dealer.

4

BUZZING BUSINESS

The drug pushers who furnish London's chemsex culture come in all shapes and sizes. Society says that a drug dealer is a villain. Popular culture portrays him as a gangster, the type of guy you don't want to be in debt to; the sort of person who might do terrible things to someone for encroaching on his patch, and in London there are many patches. But the reality of the situation is quite different, and the scale at which drug dealers operate can be dramatically different, too.

Some dealers base themselves at home, operating exclusively within the walls of their own apartments, only granting entry to those whom they know, and who are therefore not a threat. Some dealers prefer to work on a roaming basis only, never staying still for long, always hopping on the Tube or in an Uber to the address of the next customer. There are those who work as 'one-man bands', and then there are the guys who run complex logistical operations involving couriers or runners. Regardless of whose number you have in your phonebook, and let's face it we all have a few, the substances associated with chemsex can be sourced quickly and easily. And, generally speaking, the drugs these different dealers provide all come from the same higher-level suppliers – they even cost the same, give or take the odd fiver.

What is it that separates one drug dealer from another? Just one thing: reliability. And it's easy to understand why sometimes things can become difficult.

Frankie is a dealer based in Clapham. He supplies Tina, mephedrone and G to an exclusively gay customer base in his local neighbourhood and the surrounding boroughs.

Through the week it's fine, but once Thursday arrives my phone won't stop until Sunday night. I get a handful of hours of sleep during the day and I normally have to top up my stock at some point during the weekend. I would get what I felt was enough on a Thursday, but some weekends the demand is so high that if I were travelling around these streets with a backpack on with everything in it, I'd be stupid.

Frankie, like most dealers, also sells Viagra at four for £10 and Valium at two for £5, as well as the accessories that accompany his menu offerings – things like glass pipes to smoke Tina, and needles if people intend to inject.

The busiest period throughout the weekend is probably the twelve hours from Saturday evening, say about eleven o' clock, through to Sunday morning. I'll do a few drop-offs near the bars in Clapham; that's a bit of a fuck-around because people are impatient when they're pissed and because I don't want to say to five different people, who might all be in the same bar, to come to the pick-up point at the same time for obvious reasons. So, I have to text one of them: he'll take ten mins to slip away and get to me down the street. Then I'll text the next, but give him a slightly different location. It's a fucking nightmare. That sort of drop-off, and I might do three of them though the course of a Saturday night, always takes longer than I plan for it to, which pisses the next guy off, who could be a guy in Stockwell who's just opening a sex party and needs some chems to get things going. It can be a bit of a balancing act some nights.

I can feel the frustration that I have felt on a number of occasions returning to me: the same frustration I felt while waiting for a dealer to turn up to a bar or club, or most usually to my flat. But hearing Frankie acknowledge how tricky the logistics behind a typical Saturday night can be for him, I also experience a strange sense of empathy.

And it only gets worse as the hours pass by. Every time I drop off at a party, the guys are always nice. 'Are you staying for a shot?' is something I'm asked every time. And I like G just as much as the rest of them. So, I say yes. Then I'll do a bit of Tina, because let's face it, how am I going to stay awake dropping off supplies to you lot without any of the good stuff keeping me going? So, yeah, come a few hours later, I'm just as fucked as everyone else who's been up for days partying, and guess what, I start to forget who's next in the queue. I forget that I said I'd be there in twenty mins; I forget that I need to get more supplies, either from my flat or at my supplier's. That's when I'm unreliable. But what are you going to do? Sack me? Leave me a bad review somewhere? It's one of the few jobs that you can get away with being a cunt.

Nothing Frankie reveals to me comes as a big surprise. And when he mentions that customers constantly offer him a shot or a puff of Tina, it makes sense that this is a regular occurrence; after all, Frankie is a good-looking, confident and fit young man. On the few occasions when he's turned up at my place to supply a party, a lot of people's eyes have lit up, and it's fair to say that people soon come round to the idea of Frankie sticking around and getting involved in whatever it is that's going down.

Yes, I do if the group is right. Wouldn't you? I turned up at yours once and ended up messing around with two guys in your bathroom. I can't remember if I had a drop-off after you that particular night, but it's likely I did, and it's likely I was a couple of hours later than I said I would be.

Frankie only delivers; in fact, I don't know exactly where he lives, other than somewhere in Clapham. 'I don't give my address to anyone. Would you?' Frankie responds. I ask him if he has a normal job; maybe he does this drug dealing to make a couple of quid while between jobs? But again, he's deliberately aloof.

I work. I do this and that. But come Monday, I need to sleep, so that's always how I spend my Mondays. I do a few drop-offs in the evening and on Tuesday, but that's only to the die-hard Tina addicts. Wednesdays are quiet too, but Thursdays people are planning for the weekend or, in the gay world, hitting the bars. I stock up on a Thursday for the first part of the weekend rush.

I don't believe Frankie does have what I just described as a 'normal job'. I don't think he needs one. Given the account of his typical week, it's difficult to spot where in his diary he has time to do anything other than the work he's told me about. So, if that is the case, whatever mark-up he makes on the buying and selling to his client base, which is limited to the surrounding boroughs of his home, it must be enough to sustain a life in the reasonably affluent neighbourhood of Clapham.

It's not as complex or shady as a lot of people think. I know that there's a bit of chat out there about dealers watering G down. And that's true, but not to the extent I've heard some people suggest. It goes with the territory, and if people are pissed off with the quality of the stuff I provide, they've decided not to complain, at least not to my face anyway. I don't get complaints.

'But just how much is, say, G watered down?' I ask.

I have two lots of G: the stuff I give to my regulars, which is the stuff I use myself, and the stuff I keep in another bottle, which is slightly watered down. That's for the one-offs, or the new guys who ask me for chems on Grindr. By the time you're in my phonebook, I've upgraded you to the better stuff.'

For a tiny moment, I want to ask how long I was on his poorer-quality list, but think better of it.

'But the watered-down stuff is only slightly less better quality than the purer, more clean stuff,' Frankie tells me.

I ask Frankie how much he earns on an average weekend.

'How much money do I take over the weekend? Well, it varies. But let's look at the last time I dropped off at yours. I think you had six or seven guys there?'

I can't remember, and I'm fairly impressed that he can.

'You took a bag of mephedrone each,' Frankie says. 'You probably took a 50ml bottle of G too, and the guys all had V. Does that sound right?'

'I think so,' I say, agreeing more to humour him than anything else. Where is he going with all this?

Well, that's £140 for the meph; call it another £30 for the G,' Frankie says. 'Let's say another £10 for the Viagra, that's £180 in total from your little gathering. If someone wanted Tina it would be more, obviously. On a typical Saturday and Sunday, I'll do ten of those. I go to one guy's place in Kennington and there are always around thirty people there; I go every other weekend like clockwork. Do the maths for yourself.'

'But what's the profit margin?' I ask.

Frankie at this point picks up his phone and fiddles with it; I can see he's simply flicking through a news app.

'It's more modest than you think. I'm not driving around in a Range Rover, am I?'

Actually, I'm certain Frankie doesn't drive around in anything.

• • •

Another dealer who has agreed to discuss his business operation with me is Adam, a forty-year-old living in Camden. The MO of his drug dealing is quite the opposite of Frankie's, who by comparison seems somewhat of a small-time dealer. From an observational standpoint, Adam is what I would term 'much more major' in his work, yet he never seems to leave his apartment to deal. People come to him and he has a trusted aide whom he sends out into the night on a scooter. When I lived in nearby Kentish Town, I used to occasionally call in at Adam's to pick stuff up, but I never gave much thought to the business he was operating. Of course, distributing illicit drugs and collecting them don't offer themselves as conversational topics between concerned parties.

But as part of the research for this book, Adam allowed me to hang out with him at his apartment on a Friday night, so that I could witness at first hand what a typical weekend for him consisted of, and also catch a glimpse of the many, many custom-ers who passed through his door. The experience was fascinating.

Adam asked me to arrive at 9 p.m. I didn't want to be late, as, quite honestly, it had taken me a while to get him on board with the project. He had been rightly suspicious, even changing his mind once about whether to allow me access. After promising complete anonymity, guaranteeing him a name change and al-tering the true location of his apartment, he became satisfied.

After knocking on his door, having WhatsApped him only five minutes earlier, and Adam having greeted me, I become aware that there are already other people inside the flat.

'Can you just occupy yourself in my living room while I sort the guys in the kitchen out?' Adam asks me.

His customers are a man and woman, both in their twenties. From my position in the living room, with the door ajar, I can hear them talking about buying cocaine. The deal is a fairly straightforward one, and only a few minutes later, Adam rejoins me in the living room.

'It's already busy tonight,' Adam says. 'Just before it gets silly, though, if I ask you to go, don't be offended. Is that going to be an issue?'

I'm a little unprepared for this new rule, but realise I'm in no position to complain.

'And another thing, can you not get into conversations with people. I don't like people hanging around for long. If I ask someone to stay for a bit, it's my call.'

I have zero intention of engaging with anybody, and even less desire for a casual chit-chat. But I can tell Adam isn't wholly happy. There's nothing I can do at this point other than smile and agree to anything he asks. I know from an incident in the past that Adam is down the line. He's not bothered for one minute about customer service: if you dare mess with him, he'll bar you from knocking on his door. I wonder, and later I'll ask him, if he's ever worried that someone will tip off the police about the activities that go on in his property. I'm not sure I would be able to sleep at night if I were in the position he is.

The doorbell rings, and for some reason I jump slightly.

'Go and sit in the kitchen, drink something and look normal,' Adam tells me.

The new customer is in his mid-twenties, slim and has a tiny bit of stubble around his chin. He's wearing a baseball cap and a hoodie. Entering the kitchen, he looks me up and down, asks me if I'm all right and then pulls out a small wad of cash.

'James, can you reach into that cupboard and pass me the bottle with the blue top?'

Adam's sudden request catches me by surprise. I open the cupboard and there, sat on the shelf, is a fairly large plastic bottle with a blue top. Next to it is an identical bottle, which I can see has more liquid in it, only this bottle has a red top. Carefully, I pick up the bottle Adam has instructed me to pass over to him. The bottle contains GBL. The young guy in front of me tells Adam that it's 100 millilitres of the stuff that he wants, and within minutes, his order is bottled up in a new container. The five bags of mephedrone are folded to fit into one slightly bigger bag and, before I know it, the chap has it all crammed in his hoodie pocket and is being ushered out of the flat.

He was there for less than five minutes and £200 changed hands.

'I have about another five bags made up of mephedrone; after that things take a little bit longer because I'll have to bag them up as and when people order,' Adam explains.

A ping on his iPhone signals another order.

'This guy wants a gram of Tina and some Viagra,' Adam informs me.

A few seconds later, while he is rooting around in a bag on the floor, the doorbell rings. This time it's three guys, all well-dressed and already a little tipsy. Adam brings them into the kitchen, introduces me as his friend James, and asks me to pass him the bottle of G.

'What you guys up to tonight?' he asks them, and I chuckle to myself, realising that Adam is only asking so that I can get a better idea of how things work.

These chaps aren't the ones the WhatsApp order is for; they have called in, hoping that Adam will be dealing, as it's a Friday and they have made a safe bet. From what they tell Adam, I can glean that they're in town for dinner somewhere and are now heading to a friend's house party in Borough. I half-recognise one of them, and I'm fairly certain I know where in Borough they will be heading. Off they go and I add the two bags of mephedrone they bought, 50 millilitres of G and half a gram of Tina to the tally on the note I've created on my phone. So far, and it's been less than an hour, £450 has swapped hands in Adam's kitchen.

Two hours later, and after another half-dozen faces have passed through Adam's apartment, there's a knock on the door which prompts my host to suddenly make a fuss and fluster about, smartening himself up and making his immediate space look tidier than it was. Adam is in the sort of mild panic that people can often get into when a friend is about to arrive.

'A couple of guys are going to chill out here for a couple of hours,' Adam explains. 'We'll hang out in there,' he says, pointing to the living room.

Realising that his nature isn't to beat around the bush, I think he's telling me that I can join them, so I stand up as Adam heads off towards the front door. When he returns, there are two guys just behind him and I panic as I realise that I know one of the visitors.

'This is awkward,' the guy says to me, looking first at his mate, whom I don't know, and then at Adam.

'Oh, you know each other?' says Adam, sensing this could go one of two ways (either my mate freaks because I now know that he uses drugs too, or we both laugh it off and immediately get over it).

My friend hesitates for a moment, but then smiles.

'Yes, how are you, man? Small world, huh?'

Adam picks up a few bits and ushers us into his living room.

Interestingly, there is now a total falling off in terms of people turning up to buy chems. I can tell that Adam simply isn't responding to people's incoming calls or messages. Later he tells me that it was a self-imposed break of a couple of hours on his part. When the two guys turn up, he seems more relaxed, more chilled. The three of them spend two hours wearing shorts and watching YouTube videos, while steadily becoming more and more high. They have fun.

I don't immediately return with Adam to the kitchen when he starts to respond to requests after his break. I carry on chatting with the guys in the living room, occasionally confirming with Adam that I'm fine. At about 8 a.m., quite shattered, I leave the boys at the apartment and make my way home.

During the last couple of hours that I spent at Adam's apartment, I spoke with my friend about his chem habit, and asked him whether or not it had extended to chemsex. It had. I told him about my journey, and he told me about his. What struck me was that our friendship, which had existed for a number of years, had continued as normal; neither of us had ever mentioned the fact that we were both using. If only either of us had said something, we might have been able to support one another. We promised to stay in touch about our specific journeys through the world of chemsex.

I used to have a dealer who was extremely reliable, very reasonable and incredibly discreet: so much so that I never actually met him, and still do not know what he looks like. If I ever needed any chems, I would text him and he would then ask me to confirm an address. Within a specified time frame – and he never got his estimates wrong – a delivery guy would then turn up with my order on a motorbike. It was one hell of an efficient operation and, because of this, eventually I would only ever use him. This chap wasn't gay, and yet it was on Grindr that I originally found him. He is an example of a straight drug dealer who learned about gay men and their drug habits and then remodelled his business so that he could branch out into a new market. It's somewhat impressive.

What I find equally impressive is the fact that none of the dealers I spoke to while researching this book ever had any trouble with the police. It's astonishing because although each dealer operates in his own cautious manner, it still wouldn't take a genius to set up some sort of trap that would lead to them being caught red-handed. Yet, so far, this hasn't been the case, and not one of the guys I spoke to has any intention of halting their business ventures any time soon. Demand isn't dying, and the law isn't breathing down their necks either. There has never been a better time to be a drug dealer than right now.

But what about when things go wrong away from the immediate interaction of exchanging drugs for money? Did any of the dealers I have interacted with know of customers taking too much of the substances they've supplied and then finding themselves hospitalised, or indeed dead?

Yes, there's been a few. But I don't let it bother me. I supply the means for people to have a good time in the same way an off-licence does. Does anybody think negatively of the off-licence when someone drinks themselves to death? No, they don't… yet every off-licence in the country has played a part in someone's death, right?

Frankie has a very black-and-white outlook on life, and our chat really brings this aspect of his personality to the forefront.

There was a guy a fortnight ago. He'd been at a party, took a large shot of G from what I heard, went a bit mental, and instead of taking a step back or laying off the stuff for a few hours, he topped himself back up with another stupidly large shot. Dead. If you're going to use that shit, use it properly. I'm not going to stop selling it to people because some people are fucking idiots when it comes to dosage.

I asked Adam the same question, but he didn't want to talk about whether people he had dealt drugs to had died. But he did say something quite similar to Frankie.

'People need to be responsible for their own behaviour. There are idiots out there who think it's funny to take too much G, or to pour someone a bigger shot than they've asked for. They're cunts.'

Adam wouldn't say another word on the matter, but I could tell by the look on his face that I had touched a nerve.

When I look back on the last couple of years where I have been involved in, or at least been aware of, the chemsex scene, five or so names and faces pop into my mind. These are the names and faces of people who pushed their luck too far with G, pouring themselves too much or not correctly timing doses, and dying as a result; or people who lost their lives due to a crazy accident with G.

When people come unstuck with chems and then find themselves in need of urgent medical assistance, nine times out of ten, it's G-related: people doing too much G, either deliberately or mistakenly. I know there have been times in the past when I've confused my own dosage; somebody rushed over to me one time, panicking and telling me they'd accidentally given me double the measure I'd asked for because they had been distracted while getting me my shot. I lurched off to the bathroom and made myself sick immediately, but it still didn't prevent me from going under for two hours or so. It's in these situations that we are perhaps most exposed and at the mercy of nothing more than luck. I came out lucky and alive.

5

FRIEND LIKE ME

I'm interested in learning more about how people initially become involved with chemsex. How do they get sucked into the culture – is there any one specific reason? Surely, people don't just suddenly get a desire from out of nowhere to try it? If it's a case of someone simply stumbling across chemsex, then what was it that made them want to do it again, and again? But before I discuss other people's experiences, I'm going to tell you how I found myself in the chemsex underworld.

At the age of sixteen I joined the army, and the ten years that followed passed by in the blink of an eye. I decided to leave the army at the age of twenty-six and begin a normal life away from the military with my husband and our two dogs in a pretty little cottage in Windsor. Life was wonderful, until suddenly, my husband and I started to argue. Soon, the arguing escalated and became a daily occurrence. It didn't take long before hurting one another became something normal. Inevitably, we began to look elsewhere for affection and we soon realised that we didn't love each other and everything came to an end.

We separated; I said goodbye to him, my dogs and the life I was used to. I packed up my life and moved into a room in a big house in Camden, north London. At the age of twenty-seven I was single, pretty much for the first time in my adult life, and all the things I was used to – my own space, the freedom to do whatever I liked in my home, a companion to watch TV and do nice things with – all this had gone. I was alone.

At first, I took it all in my stride; the prospect of being single and living in a city quite excited me. But after about a month, I started to feel anxious about being alone and not having a nice house with bookcases, pets and a garden. I started to panic that I was essentially back to square one in life. I sucked it up, got on with things and let the faint worries in the back of my mind be. I didn't have too many friends. I'd always been quite inward-looking with regards to the army; most of the people I would see on a day-to-day basis were soldiers like me, and I think perhaps I didn't notice them missing from my life when I first left the forces, because I had my husband. It would be wrong to say I didn't have any companions, because I did, but I didn't have many friends who I could call up on a Friday afternoon and hastily arrange a night out with. So I made some.

On the surface, the gay scene looked the same as it had looked the last time I had frequented it. My ex-husband and I had been out every now and then in Soho, but in terms of being in London and catching up with mates and generally being a regular, it had been a while. Beneath the surface, though, I did start to notice that the scene was different in some ways from how it had been back when I was eighteen or nineteen. It just didn't feel as close-knit. People didn't seem as friendly, and everybody seemed more interested in their iPhones than anything else. I'd changed, too. Marriage had turned me into a different person. Among other things, it had made me a little selfish and somewhat narrow-minded.

In 2014, for my regular column in *Winq* magazine, I wrote a 1,200-word piece on why I thought gay saunas had had their day and should be closed. I didn't hold back, either, saying:

> For me as a gay man, the notion that there exist within our communities a series of places that actively promote the convening of gay men for participation in sex of shades various and in groups of all sizes rather revolts me – and I've been round the block a few times, believe me. I'm no prude, not even close, but the days when we gathered in clandestine fashion for the want of a network or a sexual outlet are surely long gone.

As you can imagine, the article was slated. As was I – and rightly so. The 27-year-old me, who was at the time blissfully married and living with my head in the clouds, had zero understanding of what single life for thousands of gay men in London was really like. I laugh now, thinking that in 2014 I didn't consider myself a 'prude', although I obviously was. I know I was, because the situations I found myself in just eighteen months later would have blown my narrow mind. The article was off the mark. It helped me secure further writing work, but it gave me a reputation – which has stayed with some people to this day – of being a stuck-up, middle-class arsehole. Had I known then what I know now, I would never have written it.

In the article, I highlighted what was then a prominent issue concerning saunas, which had become havens for men who wanted to take drugs. At the time, it seemed that not a month went by without a body being discovered at a sauna, the cause of death suspected to be, or actually being, drug-related. In my article, I cited the example of a man found dead in his own faeces in Manchester, using it as another reason why perhaps saunas should 'clean up their act'. Three years on, and in a completely different place in my life, I regret the brash language I used. But I'm glad to say that saunas have taken action and that most now have a zero-tolerance drug policy, which means people are no longer dying there.

But that doesn't mean they aren't dying somewhere else.

I visited saunas as research for this book and didn't see anyone using. Nor was I offered any drugs, apart from poppers. But, as David Stuart commented earlier, the introduction of mephedrone to the London gay scene has led to a clear surge in popularity in chemsex, one of the reasons being the drug's libido-enhancing qualities. With saunas getting tougher about drug use, people wanting to get high and have sex with strangers have found somewhere else to go – their own living rooms.

• • •

Anyway, back to me finding my newly single feet in London. I returned to the scene and started hitting the bars and clubs with a couple of new friends I'd made, or with people I had reconnected with. On a Saturday I'd go to XXL, which I still do occasionally, but back then, and especially as the worries started to set in about not having a guy to share my life with, I would hang out in a corner of the club where the lights were switched off for most of the night. The immediate buzz of hooking up with a stranger seemed to ease my worries, even if this fix was only temporary. Of course, if you're a happy singleton and prefer life as a solo flyer, you might not be familiar with this feeling, or it's probably not something you care too much about. But I wasn't used to that, and immediate connections, like the ones made in darkrooms or those you can forge through Grindr, eased my worries immediately. Ultimately, though, they made me feel worse.

It was in the darkroom of XXL one night that someone casually asked me if I wanted a 'bump'. He then placed under my nose a house key with some white powder on the end, told me it was 'meph' and for whatever reason, I think I just thought fuck it, I sniffed it up my nose without giving it much thought: simple as that. He returned to the task in hand and, almost immediately, I felt brilliant. I felt awesome. I'd tried cocaine in the past and had had a puff of a joint once or twice before, but I'd never really gone crazy for either. But within what must have only been minutes, I was asking this guy if I could have another go and he obliged. Nothing crazy happened. The lights came on, the music stopped and I got a cab home. But the idea, the kick and the pleasure from just those five or so bumps of this new thing called meph very much stuck in my mind.

A couple of weeks later I found myself on a date of sorts, with a handsome guy, let's call him Peter. He took me to The Ivy and it was all very posh. At the end of the evening he mentioned that his flatmates, back in whichever part of town it was that he lived, were having some friends over and that it would probably be good vibes for a party. He suggested we should go, and with that, we made our way.

There certainly was a house party going on when we arrived. Already in full swing, it was immediately exhilarating: lots of different faces – lots of handsome faces, actually – and people who were genuinely interesting. I enjoyed it from the moment I arrived. Someone handed me a beer and I did what I do best: mingled, chatted and got to know people.

An hour or so in, a guy I was in mid-conversation with subtly reached into his pocket and asked me the same question the guy in the darkroom had two weeks earlier: 'Do you want a bump?' Only this time, I didn't hesitate with my response. Knowing full well what the question meant, I said yes.

And then it hit me. I'd either not been paying attention to my surroundings properly or the other guys at the party were all being purposely coy, but I suddenly noticed that almost everyone around me was doing exactly the same thing. People were happily and casually 'bumping' away to their hearts' content while chatting, laughing, dancing and drinking. It was all so relaxed and it was brilliant, actually brilliant: the vibes, the happiness, the fun. This was a group of young professional men, letting off a bit of steam on a Friday night after a busy London week.

Companionship. If there's one thing you think you have when you're off your face in a club or at an after-party in someone's flat, surrounded by dozens and dozens of people you hardly know but who right at that moment you seem to love, it's companionship. We're all in this together. 'Who wants another fucking bump?' The environment I found myself in that night immediately appealed to my senses. These guys weren't queuing up to get into Heaven, or traipsing all over town looking for a good time or a decent bar. They ran their lives, went about their business, then piled into someone's gorgeous apartment at the weekend. What wasn't there to love about it?

My attraction to it wasn't the drugs, though; it wasn't the drugs even by half: it was the crowd. What captivated me was, and here's that word again, *companionship*. The prospect of friends was what I really got the biggest kick out of, although I would be lying if I didn't admit that I'd look at some of the guys and think to myself that they would make excellent boyfriends. But of course I was shoving so much mephedrone up my nose, a drug that had never properly worked its way into my life until then, that I had a heightened sense of belonging. As I explained earlier, meph allows you to feel an affinity with those around you; it makes you think 'everybody loves me and I love everybody around me'. And because, niggling away constantly at the back of my mind was this fear of being alone, I was captivated by this new world.

As the night went on, I saw some guys in the kitchen messing around with syringes. I assumed the worst, but my fear was short-lived. These boys weren't about to smack up; they were using the syringes, without a needle fixed, to measure out a clear liquid from a small plastic bottle. Of course, this was G. I'd clicked with a couple of guys, and Peter was keeping an eye on me from across the room to make sure I didn't get carried away and do something silly. People told me what G was, and what it typically did, and I thought, 'Hell, why not?' What happened next is crucial.

Instead of just leaving an amateur like me to get my own fix of G, bearing in mind what the consequences are of getting the measurement wrong, what those boys did – and don't forget they were strangers to me – was give me a valuable lesson on how to do G safely. They made no bones about the risks involved with taking the drug, and it's a lesson I have passed on to others a couple of times myself. If somebody is going to do G, learning how to do it right is paramount. These guys were good guys. Some of them are still my friends today, and the ones who are wouldn't think twice about calling someone out for not following these rules, rules that are there to stop you from accidentally killing yourself – or someone else. I took the 'shot', so called because it's usually taken in a small glass, with a little bit of mixer, normally a soft drink, to take away the terrible fucking taste of raw G.

I have never been as confident in making a statement as the

one I am about to make: I developed an addiction of sorts to G from just that one shot.

I *loved* it!

Within about ten minutes my head was spinning like crazy; I was on top of the world; I felt euphoric; G made me move; I was dancing away to the music like nobody was watching me. The way G made me feel for about an hour was enough for me to want to do it as much as I possibly could. I liked it so much that when the time did eventually come for me to stop using it, I needed real support not just from drug counsellors but also from friends, family and colleagues. But right then, at that precise moment, it didn't matter. This new thing, G, became my favourite thing in the world. I was at that party for twenty-four hours. Time just seemed to pass us all by in our intoxicated states; life in the world outside continued but for us thirty or so guys at the apartment, time stood still.

Following this introduction to the chemsex scene, taking drugs and partying for days on end in the relative safety of someone's apartment became my preferred choice of weekend activity; so much so that the partying occasionally spilled over to a Monday, or even a Tuesday. Away from London and married, I had been oblivious to this culture and its popularity. My time in the army had been wholeheartedly anti-drugs in nature; my piss could and would be tested often. I had never had any desire to try anything other than booze. This all changed for me pretty much overnight, and the change can be pinpointed directly to the night I met Peter.

Three months later, I'd cut from my life anyone who wasn't also into spending days and days on these substances and letting go of life for a bit. But it's important here for me to point out that the activities I had become more and more involved in were not motivated by a desire for sex. The key factor was my desire to keep going: to dance some more and unwind; to carry on chatting with all these nice men, who were the kind of guys I wanted to be around.

It was following a party at some stranger's flat one Sunday morning, after we'd all partied at East Bloc or somewhere, that I crossed a new boundary. I agreed to go along to another place where I was told people would be 'a little more relaxed, where the vibe would be a little different'. I was being introduced to something more than a chill-out; I was going to a chemsex party.

Remember that I explained how great those drugs made me feel the first time I tried them? Now imagine me experiencing those same powerful feelings again – then add the prospect of sex, lots and lots of sex. I was like a kid in a sweet shop. I really was. And the sad part is that I started hanging out less and less with a lot of those nice guys I'd met and done casual chill-outs with, and instead I began knocking around with a crowd that was mostly just interested in sex. I was on a slippery slope towards self-destruction.

On the face of it, it looks as if my fears of being alone fuelled my exploration of the chill-out scene and that this simply snowballed into me then trying chemsex. But were there any other motivating factors that we should consider?

Greg Owen is a well-known and respected campaigner within the gay community in London. It is largely thanks to him that people now have access to PrEP, the revolutionary medication they can take once a day to massively reduce their risk of catching HIV. Greg co-founded the website iwantPrEP-now.co.uk and is one of the most vocal activists for PrEP in the UK. But before his busy life of campaigning and championing the life-changing effects of PrEP, Greg, like many of us, was a chemsex addict.

I'd always done drugs on the scene, you know, MDMA and a bit of G in the clubs in Vauxhall with my ex-boyfriend. But around 2009, they all just got shit. The drugs were crap ... it was impossible to get high and have a good time like we had been used to. They were a waste of money.

And then mephedrone arrived. And it was good. The stuff we were sniffing back in 2009, 2010 was a million miles away from the shit that's on the scene now ... Mephedrone back then was good. But alongside this, my ex started playing away. I didn't know initially, but while he was fucking around with other guys, he discovered crystal meth. He smoked it while fucking some guys and really took to it. He came home and introduced it into our own sex life. We now had Tina and this new wonder drug, mephedrone. But he kept cheating, messing with other guys away from our relationship. And he became HIV-positive. That was a really emotional time for me; it really fucked with my mind. It's not a nice story, but the toll it took on our relationship led to some dark times, and that involved domestic violence.

I was in a mess, so he started to look elsewhere too. We broke up and I started hanging out in groups or with couples and when I did, I carried on doing crystal meth and mephedrone. It all snowballed from there.

Greg's story highlights some of the key reasons why he became involved in chemsex, but perhaps the most crucial of these was the emergence of mephedrone. Greg had had a taste for drugs before meph, but he and a lot of other people were growing frustrated by the lack of quality found in the substances being pushed around London's gay clubs. His route into the chemsex culture was in some sense born out of his frustration with other drugs. Back when Greg first became involved in the scene, we were coming out of a recession. The period won't be remembered as being a particularly affluent one and the same holds true for the gay clubbing community. I believe that the cost of a night out is a key reason why people now choose to forgo clubs and bars, and instead order in a shit-load of gear and throw a house party – no transport costs, no expensive bar bills and no hassle of dealing with a crowd. Greg tells me that the same was true back in his day:

'It was fucking expensive. A night out was not a cheap

exercise. And people didn't have as much cash. Meph was dirt cheap, it gave you a hell of a kick and it facilitated horny sex. What wasn't there to love about it?'

But let's move away from Greg for a while and turn our attention to Calvin. He's a friend of mine who I'd thought was outside the chemsex scene but who, unbeknownst to me, was secretly battling his own addiction to chemsex.

Calvin tells me it all began when he dabbled with new drugs, having already been a user of others.

'It's fair to say I got into chemsex simply by graduating from ecstasy, then cocaine and then ketamine. I got into G, then Tina and of course, and like everybody did, mephedrone.'

But then Calvin tells me about something that was central to his descent into addiction, something we've heard before:

My relationship stopped me from really getting stuck in a rut of doing drugs and having sex with lots of people. But then, quite out of the blue, my relationship was over. There was no stopping me then. Chems got their grip around me and I started having sex with lots of people, facilitated by lots of drugs.

Although, in a way, Greg's and Calvin's introductions to chemsex were different to mine, we all share something in common. Can the stress and emotional fallout of breaking up with someone you love be enough to make you step out of your comfort zone and enter a different, darker world? Did Greg and Calvin, like me, both recoil at the prospect of loneliness and then actively fight against it, shielding themselves with lots of people, lots of sex and lots of intimacy?

I want to know if this is a culture-wide thing. Are people afraid of living a life of loneliness and is this fear causing them to dive head first into recklessness? I returned to David Stuart at 56 Dean Street to find out.

Our data suggests that chemsex use that might have been non-problematic or recreational becomes excessive and problematic following the break-up of a relationship. People emerging from long-term relationships struggle especially, as they find themselves single, out of practice in regard to dating, and poorly equipped for the big city, app-focused, disposable casual sex scene that differs so enormously from the days before their relationship.

The break-ups that Calvin, Greg and I suffered, and the insight provided by David Stuart, support the idea that a big, emotional event can trigger some behavioural characteristics that make chemsex participants more likely to want to engage in the culture. But I'm not about to throw the towel in here – I can blame my ex for a lot of things, but I'm not about to blame him for my chemsex life. There must be more to it.

When I look back, I can see a number of factors that were pivotal to my own experiences. It wasn't just loneliness; there were other things too – things ranging from self-esteem issues to general boredom.

And there was also technology.

We carry around with us an invention that allows us to do pretty much anything we like. We can now use our phones to secure a mortgage in the comfort of our own homes; not too long ago we'd have had to make an appointment with the bank manager and get a medical. These days we can transfer money to someone in Australia, or go shopping when and where we want; we can send birthday cards at our own convenience; we can order dinner; share our views about the latest news in the world – even make news ourselves via a platform like Twitter. Just one invention lets us do all of these things with ease: the internet.

And the internet also allows us to socialise. I probably speak to more people on a day-to-day basis via apps like Grindr than I actually do in person. From the comfort of my armchair, I can talk to dozens of people at once and arrange an intimate liaison. I just send some well-filtered and slim-looking images of myself from four years ago, convince the guy (or guys) to come over, immediately get down to business and then be left to my night in front of the TV alone; satisfied because I've been laid, and what's more have not spent a penny or had to make any real effort. But this semi-virtual world where thousands of connections are made every day also lends itself to something else: an unpoliced environment where drug dealers can advertise products. Where I live, in south London, hook-up apps offer the quickest and easiest way to get your hands on some drugs.

Let's just take stock of the situation for a second. What we have here – if we imagine me on a Sunday afternoon in my apartment, feeling bored and a little bit frisky – is me holding enough rope to hang myself with. I can call around a couple of local gays, although of course I would have to qualify them before getting them over; I'd need to check they were 'open-minded' and 'up for chilling out'. Once that's cracked, though, I can then go to one of the handful of drug pushers operating within a mile or so of me, respond to the 'Shop Open' or 'TMCGV' invitations and, boom! I've got myself a party. If apps like Grindr didn't exist, it would be impossible for me to organise any of these meetings. Finally, and also thanks to the wonders of modern technology, I can get to places quickly, or get people quickly to me, due to the services now provided by companies like Uber – it's all just too easy. Some dealers depend on this last factor, Uber, as central to their business operation.

The planets have aligned somewhat to help chemsex culture take hold in London. Consider the desire that people have to find connections and companionship – and the ease with which they can do this, thanks to apps like Scruff and Grindr. Then examine the way dealers have centralised their business oper- ations in these same spaces, and look at the cost-effectiveness of the three popular drugs that are fundamental to chemsex. What you have are means, motive and opportunity. These come together to create a catalyst, forging a resculpting of drug-use habits for many, and an easy route in for others who are looking to fill a void in their lives.

6

BLURRED LINES

Matt Cain, *The Independent*, Saturday 17 October 2015:

It's Friday night and a group of gay men is gathering in London for a party in one of their homes. They're of different ages and backgrounds but all are in the professions, many of them affluent and enviably successful. The party has been arranged via Grindr and other sexual-networking apps – and it will last for the whole weekend. It begins when the men strip to their underwear, watch porn and then snort, swallow or 'slam' (inject) drugs until they're overwhelmed by the urge to have sex.

I've never been attracted to chemsex, but a couple of my friends are. They're in their late twenties and early thirties and both have successful media careers. A while ago I noticed that after attending parties they were often too exhausted to go to work on Monday and spent most of the following week plagued by depression, anxiety and paranoia. When I expressed my concerns, they insisted they were just having fun and I was accused of morally judging them. Nevertheless, I started to become seriously worried when one of them told me that at a recent party he had misjudged his dose of G, gone under and had come round three hours later to discover someone was having unprotected sex with him.

Matt Cain, now editor-in-chief of *Attitude* magazine, wrote this article to coincide with the release of *Chemsex*, a film made by two journalists at *Vice* magazine. The film was raw in nature and groundbreaking in the way it acted as a window into some of the more sinister elements of chemsex culture. In 2014 and 2015, several newspapers ran articles on the chemsex scene. But these were written by people who had never really experienced the lifestyle at first hand and were often and sensationalist. There was very much a 'look at what the gays are doing now' undertone to several of the pieces, and I feel that all this did was encourage those of us involved in chemsex to do it even more: a defiant 'fuck you', if you like. But I can't say the same is true of Matt Cain's reporting. The person Matt is talking about in his article, the person who loses control, goes under on some G and wakes up to find someone having sex with him, is me. I'm the person who told Matt that I had been raped.

It happened at the end of the August bank holiday weekend in 2015; it had been three days of nothing but partying for me and ended with about fifteen completely random people in my flat. It started in a popular bar in Vauxhall, then progressed to a major nightclub well-known among London's gay partygoers and then finally, at about 10.30 a.m. on the Monday morning,

I dragged the people around me at the club to my apartment. I didn't know any of them. A dealer arrived shortly after to furnish us and we carried on partying. Roughly twenty-four hours later, I woke up in my bedroom with zero recollection of how I had got there.

This isn't the only time I have ever overdosed. In fact, a friend once filmed me going under, swirling around on the floor in my own private world, being annoying and looking like a complete dick. He wanted to teach me a lesson that I would learn when I eventually came around.

But let's get back to that bank holiday weekend in 2015, and me finally waking up in my bed at home. I realised almost immediately that I wasn't alone. An overweight Turkish man was having sex with me. He had been fucking me for God knows how long, but as going-under episodes typically last for at least an hour, often longer, I figured that this guy had been having sex with me for some time without my consent. I went fucking crazy. Everybody was ordered to leave the flat and I had more than just a go at my flatmate; in fact, he didn't remain my flatmate for very long after that. Someone at the party had invited the Turkish guy over on Grindr without my knowledge and, finding me in my bed soon after his arrival, he thought it open season to help himself as I lay in a deep G-induced sleep in the darkness of my bedroom. Pretty grim, huh?

I didn't report the incident to the police. How could I? I figured that if I did I'd have to tell them exactly how and why the perpetrator had happened to be at my house. I would have had to tell the police officers that I'd been taking a number of drugs for a number of days and, by coincidence, so had all the other people with me. Surely the police would want to know names? I didn't want the local plods to associate my address with drugs ranging in all classes. No, I couldn't possibly call the police.

I felt deflated and I also felt guilty that I'd brought the situation largely upon myself. I was worried about the consequences of the guy having had unprotected sex with me. I was so scared about having to tell people that I'd been hosting a sex party when the incident happened that I didn't even access PEP (post-exposure prophylaxis), which was incredibly stupid of me, but that was my mindset at the time. I also had the comedown from hell to deal with, which made the entire situation a million times worse. I thought my mother would disown me and be disgusted with the position I'd put myself in, and what if it all got out? It's not big-headed to say that I have a profile; when my first book came out, it made the front page of the *Daily Mail*. What would all those people who had sent me such nice letters think?

All these scary thoughts went through my mind constantly for days and I truly hated myself. Of course, I know now that the paranoia associated with a mephedrone comedown was compounding the difficulties of my situation. I had nobody to talk to, and apart from Matt, who is one of my closest friends, I still haven't talked to anybody else about it. It's now something that happened to me and I just have to accept it. Did it stop me from putting myself in those situations again? No. But it was an early battle scar in what became a fairly drawn-out conflict for me personally as I struggled to combat something that was clearly harming me. It was the moment when I realised that what I was doing was hurting me. I didn't think then, and I still don't think now, that chemsex was wrong and that the people doing it were, or are, bad. But at that particular time in my life, crying alone for days in my flat, I knew it really wasn't for me. Or maybe I wasn't really for it.

I have since had conversations on a number of occasions with other people who have told me a similar story to mine. In fact, no fewer than four friends have confided in me that they have woken up during, or found out later, that they'd been sexually assaulted while being 'under'. On every occasion, the drug that made them go under was G.

G is referred to as a date-rape drug, specifically because it can render you unconscious if you take too much. Every time I have gone under, my first thought when I've woken up has been: I could quite easily have died. And the grim truth is that I would never have even known that I was dying: with a G overdose you just fall asleep and your heart stops.

I was eager to find out if the instance of me and my four unnamed friends being separately raped was an anomaly, a freak coincidence. And there was no better person to ask than 56 Dean Street's David Stuart. I asked him how often he saw people at his London clinic who displayed concerns about losing the ability to give consent.

I think the more disturbing question is: how many of my patients do not display concerns about losing the power to give consent? I think the concept of what consent means within the highly charged, super-intoxicated chemsex environment is blurry at best, traumatic as a given, fatal at its worst. Often there's an urgent desire to 'fit in', to avoid rejection, almost – almost – at any cost. Imagine saying yes to the invitation to attend a chemmed-up orgy, regardless of who is there. Imagine saying yes to whatever drugs are available there. Imagine saying yes to the second dose of GBL being offered, or the offer of a charged syringe, if it promises to get you higher and make you feel sexier in this environment. Imagine not feeling sexy enough in this environment. Say yes to the drugs, and that will fix that.

Then imagine saying no to someone you don't want to have sex with for... for any reason. The reason should not matter; no means no in any other environment. But what does 'no' mean in this environment? How will it be perceived, after all the times 'yes' has been uttered? Will it be respected? Would you have the courage to say no? How high are you? Too high to know what you want? Too high to assess your own desires, to assess your own safety? Too high to respect your own boundaries? Too high to weigh the consequences of your actions? And even if you were able to assess and consent in this state, and in this environment, who around you is first to say: 'You know what, you're really high right now, I'd rather wait till you're a little more together before going further'? Should we be expecting that of someone who's highly intoxicated, possibly not slept in a day or two?

I hope there are many guys out there who are conscious of their own emotional needs, as well as those with them, even when enjoying the chem high. I hope there are lots of guys who refuse to shag someone who is a little too intoxicated to be consenting to sex. I'm sure there are many. But the words I hear most in clinics, I'm devastated to say, are: 'I really regret the sex I had yesterday, but it's my own fault. I put myself in that situation, I took too many drugs. That wasn't assault, it was my own fault.'

A conversation about consent and what it means to a vulnerable population of people, seeking sexual and social affirmation in a high-risk environment and intoxicated by some very powerful drugs, is a minefield of complicated issues. But one that, very urgently, needs to be had. By our whole community.

Why is it that people prefer to talk in confidence to a counsellor like David, instead of picking up the phone and dialling 999? I want to ask the police if there are any grounds for a person to fear the worst when reporting a sexual assault where drug use is involved. Would the police overlook the circumstances and deal with the matter reported?

Using the official online resource for policing in England and Wales – Ask the Police – I asked the Metropolitan Police Service whether a person should have any legitimate worries about making an allegation of sexual assault which involved them also having to explain the circumstances surrounding the incident, including the use of illegal drugs. Would they find themselves encountering any sort of trouble relating to the admission of the drug use? The police provided this response:

> If the person admits to taking drugs, the police may consider taking action against him for possession of drugs, but generally the police and CPS [Crown Prosecution Service] do not aim to prosecute victims, and may decide it is not in the public interest in the circumstances. Additionally, if he had taken the only drugs that were in his possession, it is likely the police will be unable to proceed with such a prosecution due to lack of evidence. Although it is technically possible to proceed with a charge of possession where the substance has already been consumed, from a practical point of view, there can be problems. For example, substances are normally subjected to testing prior to charging to determine what class of drug was taken, which will not be possible.

So, the official police response doesn't provide a solid 'yes' or 'no' answer. It underlines the fact that the situation is murky. It's important to emphasise words such as 'may' and 'generally', and then consider what the person in this situation will be thinking: 'Might I get in trouble?' and 'What if I'm arrested?'

Using the same Ask the Police service, I asked what sort of guidance the police give about incidents of consent and where drugs, once again, are a contributing factor. This time the police response was a little clearer:

It would really depend on the facts in each case as to whether a person lost the capacity to consent, but it is possible to lose the capacity to consent through drugs/alcohol: see R v. Bree 2007, where it was held that a temporary loss of capacity to choose whether to have sexual intercourse, through consumption of alcohol or any other reason, means consent is not present.

R v. BREE 2007

B and the victim M had consumed a considerable amount of alcohol during an evening spent together. They had then returned to B's flat and had sexual intercourse. B was later arrested and charged with raping M.

Initially, the prosecution argued that M had not had the capacity to consent to intercourse, as a result of her being unconscious during most of the sexual activity that had occurred. However, after evidence given during the course of the trial this argument was changed to assert that despite her ability to thwart B's sexual advances being impaired by the alcohol, she did have the capacity to consent and she had as far as she had been able made it clear to B that she hadn't wished to have sexual intercourse. M agreed that her memory was not particularly clear as to exactly what had happened, but she did recall that she had not actually said 'no' to sexual intercourse but was sure that she had not consented. B argued that she had been conscious during the incident and that he had reasonably believed that she had consented.

B was convicted of rape and appealed on the issue of consent. The police response continued:

> Consent is defined in Section 74 of the Sexual Offences Act 2003 and if, as a result of consuming alcohol or for any other reason, capacity to choose whether to have sexual intercourse is temporarily lost, then no consent was present and dependent upon enquiries into the state of mind of the 'victim' if intercourse takes place, then it would be rape.
>
> Conversely, where a complainant voluntarily consumes a large amount of alcohol but remains capable of consenting to sexual intercourse and consents to do so then that cannot be said to be rape.
>
> It should be noted, however, that in either scenario capacity to consent could be lost prior to any loss of consciousness but that would be dependent upon the state of mind of any given individual involved in the situation at the time. No measure should be put upon the amount of alcohol that could be consumed before reaching that level as every person handles alcohol and its effects in different ways.
>
> The definition of consent in Section 74 of the 2003 Act for the purpose of the offence of rape is sufficiently addressed for situations involving alcohol consumption by reference to 'capacity to make that choice'.

Too frequently on the TV news, we see reports of people who have had the confidence to make allegations of rape and who are then subjected to rigorous cross-examination, and are often painted as villains. A lawyer friend told me candidly that his number one task when defending a client at a trial is to discredit the reliability of a witness, and if it's accepted that the key witness was using drugs at the time of an alleged offence, 'I'm going to place that central to my approach. I'd rip them to pieces.'

This probability piles yet more pressure on the shoulders of somebody who's facing personal uncertainty about taking just the first step in reporting a sexual offence. In light of these major factors – that the police 'may' want to act against victims for using or possessing drugs, and that the most probable outcome in court, if it gets that far, is that an articulate barrister will trash your character – gay men who are raped while having chemsex simply prefer to keep their mouths shut. Silent witnesses. This shocking situation is fundamentally due to a failure by the justice sector in this country. These people are alone; they don't pick up the phone and they are left having to accept the situation as it stands.

Although the police profess to being open-minded where drug use and sexual assault are concerned, for whatever reason, the gay community doesn't believe them. We think we'll be treated like criminals. And even with the police guidance that consent cannot always be present when external influences like alcohol and drugs are factored into the equation, we still doubt the CPS will progress our complaints to trial. Even if it does, we fear the wrath of defence barristers as they serve up an old-fashioned: 'You wanted it, didn't you? You had taken drugs.'

And we simply don't have the capacity to deal with that. Remember my lawyer friend's direct words: 'I'd rip them to pieces.' The 'them' he's referring to are victims of a rape ordeal.

And who can blame us gays for this? We all know about the historic anti-gay hostility of police officers during anti-Section 28 marches: you can YouTube footage of police officers beating young gay men on the capital's streets with batons. There's a reason why police LGBT liaison groups exist. And who can overlook the catastrophic failures of the Metropolitan Police in their handling of the Stephen Port serial killer case? The police may say they are an all-inclusive force for good, but it's easy to understand why many people don't believe them. This is something the police must address now.

It's because of this fear of repercussion, it's because the police have failed to make the case for openness and compassion towards what is a huge issue within the gay community of London, that people have been able to carry out serial rapes without fear of consequences. There is, right now, an unpunished group of sex offenders who are getting away with it because of some unfortunate victim circumstances. They are planning their next attacks, because they know where to find their victims. This is due to police officers, and beyond that the criminal justice system, not having any proper understanding, compassion or respect for gay men who take drugs and who find themselves the victims of sex assaults. Shame.

Stephen Morris is a forensic psychotherapist with the National Probation Service. His work is focused on the rehabilitation of offenders of sexual offences, typically once they have been found guilty and have begun their sentence. I met him for a coffee near his Borough offices in central London, to learn more about the people he works with, and to find out whether or not he sees chemsex as a feature in the cases of any of his offenders.

The National Probation Service is only just becoming aware of the issue of chemsex and is at the very early stages of developing an effective and compassionate response. A year ago we did not even have a language to describe what we were witnessing; this is now changing. Sadly, it is not until high-profile cases make the headlines that agencies are prompted to give adequate consideration. In London, I started recognising the issue in my clinical work about eight years ago. I have been fortunate indeed that my managers have responded positively to my concerns and I am now able to consult with probation officers across London, assisting them in the sentence planning and face-to-face work with the men they are working with. I write and advise on assessment and pre-sentence reports for the courts; these reports assist the courts to understand the case before them and advise on sentencing.

A couple of years ago, I'd hardly ever see young gay men coming through the criminal justice system or entering the re-habilitation programme for sex offences they had committed. It was very rare. Today, I see at least one each time we begin a new treatment programme, which is monthly.

On a monthly basis, Stephen starts a programme with about

nine or ten recently sentenced men across London, with offenders including paedophiles and rapists. When quizzed about his gay offenders and the circumstances surrounding their respective offences, he stresses that he cannot talk about individual cases specifically, but generally speaking, chems and chemsex are more often than not contributory elements.

Chems have started to feature in many cases. When you have been awake for three days straight, and then when you factor in the psychological effects of substances like Tina and meph, an episode of psychosis is highly likely. When that happens, some people have no understanding of the behaviour they are engaging in. I often work with offenders who have zero recollection of committing their crimes. Equally, they may also be victims of sexual crime. Again, they have a sense that something has happened to them while under the influence of substances, but their recall is vague, adding to their distress and trauma.

I ask him if it is possible to look at these people with some compassion.

Yes, of course you can; crime is often a communication of something that cannot be said. Behind sexual crime there is more often than not a story of trauma, pain, deprivation, abuse, self-hatred and suffering. If the offender is gay then you can add to that list experiences of rejection, shame, guilt, bullying, identity issues and self-loathing. For many who commit sexual

84

offences, these experiences feature significantly throughout their lives, not as one-off experiences but as ongoing daily events. No one can endure such psychological torture without seeking resource for relief and increasingly that relief is found in chems, chemsex and problematic sexual behaviour.

Does it make what they did OK?

No, it doesn't at all. If they are guilty of a sexual crime they must face the full consequences of justice. However, justice must also be compassionate and provide the understanding and help they need so that the behaviour stops and no more victims are created. In my opinion, it is naïve beyond belief to think that the response to people who commit sexual offences should be devoid of compassion. To not meet their behaviour with compassion would be to repeat the very factors that caused the problem in the first place.

While chatting with Stephen, I tell him about a conversation I had with someone who was asked to do something quite extraordinary at a sex party he attended in December 2016. Sam told me that he went along to a guy's flat in Clapham at which the planned premise was that a guy in his early twenties would be there and was looking to exclusively be the 'bottom' in the group's activity. The other attendees were all tops. Sam continued:

He was there for the specific reason of being a bottom; he wanted to experience being fucked by a number of different guys. It was consensual to the extent of it being arranged in advance and him being aware there was a group of people there who all would, as desired, have sex with him. He'd even hand-picked some of the guys specifically.

So far so good, but Sam went on to say: 'After an hour or so of taking meph and a shot or two of G, he became a little paranoid about the whole situation and asked me if I would act as a sensible bystander, intervening if and when things got too heavy.' Essentially, the guy was placing consent into someone else's hands. I want to know if Stephen has witnessed this in his work and if so, from a judicial perspective, is it ethical to take a third-party point of view on consent? Interventions notwithstanding, how can two people have the same boundaries in terms of what's OK, and what's not? Stephen tells me:

Asking someone to keep a look out and 'step in' if things are becoming unsafe is a good idea in practice and in managing an immediate risky situation. However, legally each person present would be held responsible for their own behaviour and I doubt if a collective responsibility would be recognised by the courts. It would be more than likely that if something happened then all present could be implicated by association. This fact is hardly recognised at all by those hosting chill-outs. The vulnerability of all involved is not something people appear to be recognising at all. If you invite a stranger to your home, or a group of strangers, you have no idea of their psychological state or mental health. They may have been high for many hours, and moving in and out of a psychotic state; the only way you will know is when they totally lose it, and then it is too late. To have someone acutely mentally ill in your living room, or sexually assaulting people, or downloading images of child abuse on your laptop, immediately implicates you in the crime. These are the situations that are occurring and bringing gay men into prison and probation who only a few years ago we would never have seen.

Stephen's message here strikes an interesting chord. Even from my own experiences, I know I have had countless strangers in my apartment many times who, quite frankly, I didn't know from Adam. This is the norm for the chill-out and chemsex scenes. When else would you let a stranger into your home like this? And given that this is commonplace in the chemsex world, can we really be surprised to see the issue of consent rising so much, and more gay men finding themselves on the wrong side of the law as a result? According to Stephen:

The issue of consent is at the heart of sexual crime and sexual crime committed in the context of chemsex. The issue of consent will be at the heart of the police investigation and in any subsequent trial. In the cases I have worked with over the last few years the recognition of consent and the associated understanding by victim and perpetrator has been, on the whole, totally absent. Without consent, any sexual behaviour is a sexual crime and attracts the full range of judicial responses including custody, being on the sex offender register, being subject to police and probation monitoring in the community and being required to make full disclosure to employers, partners and families. Saying 'I did not know' is no defence. The lack of awareness of consent issues within the male gay community is frightening indeed. In the highly sexualised environments where inhibitions are reduced, many sexual assaults are occurring each weekend involving viewing images of child abuse online, joining in 'caming' rooms where sexual abuse is being streamed live, acts of inappropriate touching to violent rape of someone who is unconscious or who is so out of it that they cannot meaningfully consent. Victims often report that because they were in such a setting they did not have any right to say 'no' and perpetrators will say 'as we were all there, I thought I could do anything'. This is distorted thinking and is highly dangerous.

I ask Stephen if the offenders he works with at the Probation Service fit the bill of the typical sex offender.

Not all gay men committing sexual crime in a chemsex context set out to commit their crime. They may not have planned to commit the crime, they may not have groomed or targeted their victim, but nonetheless a sexual crime occurs and if found guilty they will face the full judicial process. There is a lack of self-care, self-worth and self-esteem within gay men that creates this vulnerability and no one appears to be saying 'no'. I blame an education system and a government that remains confused and unclear concerning sex education and especially LGBT sex education. I blame elements of the gay community and gay media who seek to shame and blame those who are associated with chemsex. Such attitudes feed into silence and secrecy. The consequences of silence and secrecy are well-documented in relation to sexual crime and, sadly, I am witnessing our own community contributing to this lethal cycle; you only have to read some of the posted comments on social media when the issue of chemsex is raised: most comments will be more toxic in effect than any substance. If the criminal justice system can offer a compassionate response, then so too can the gay community.

But how can all of this be tackled? How best do we address the problem of a growing number of gay men encountering the judicial system who, as Stephen has just pointed out, are sometimes both perpetrator and victim and who don't fit the stereotypical view of a sex offender? How can you correctly punish and rehabilitate a person if they cannot even remember committing the crime in the first place?

I also raised the matter with David Stuart from 56 Dean Street. David told me that if a clinical psychotherapist, as a result of what he sees happening in the justice system every day, is suggesting that education across the whole gay community is needed, then a picture begins to emerge of us all being under-equipped in knowing across the board what's wrong and what's right. Can this really be the case?

There's no sex education for gay men, is there? We have to figure this world out for ourselves, and when this happens, you have varying levels of education. This is why so much pressure is on the government presently to provide young people with a proper sex and relationships education at school, in the formative years.

Stephen Morris believes that part of this education must be based on the consequences of committing a crime. He warns that for a few moments of carelessness when high, lifelong and detrimental effects are a genuine probability if somebody alleges an offence.

A rape conviction is a very serious matter, with a minimum sentence of five years in jail, and you'll also be made to sign the sex offenders' register for at least ten years. That means you'll face heavy restrictions when you rehabilitate and will have to try and pick up the pieces of your life after your sentence: you can't leave the country, it will be difficult to get a job. Rape as an offence has terrible stigma. Now think back to the moment you did that shot of G, or slammed that bit of Tina. Everyone needs to know what can happen when they cross a line… a very blurry line.

I ask Stephen what the future holds for people who have

committed sexual crimes out of character when under the influence of drugs.

The ongoing assessment of risk, provision of treatment and supporting someone through their time within the criminal justice system is also part of my work. It is the latter that is most disturbing as it is where I witness lives totally wrecked by the outcome of chemsex behaviour. It is also the area of my work where I experience most hope, as the resilience of the men who rebuild their lives is deeply inspiring. The task of all criminal justice agencies has always been to hold the wholeness of any individual. Our task remains that, while ensuring an individual faces justice, they also have opportunity for compassion and healing. No one is ever the total of their destructive or offending behaviour; those who commit crimes in the context of chemsex are no exception.

Stephen's professional experiences, and the examples he has given of just a handful of offenders, leave a question hanging over the community-wide position on boundaries and sexual consent. Everybody – you, me, your friends and your neighbours – understands what's right and wrong: we all know that no means no. But most of the time we are in full control of our minds; we are intelligent human beings who are fully responsible for the decisions we make.

When someone loses their ability to think clearly, or even to make conscious decisions, they might have been awake for three days and slamming large quantities of Tina into their veins. Their mind can take on a life of its own. It's not too dissimilar to a psychopath claiming insanity for his or her actions. The lowering of inhibitions is one of the main known side effects of meph, meth and G. Although it is in no way an excuse for their actions, it's perhaps understandable that people who are heavily under the influence of certain drugs may do things they would never do when sober. Perhaps we need to do more to educate people about the risks of lowering their inhibitions. To warn them of what can happen if they ever lose control. Rape is an unspeakably cruel crime, and an emphasis must be placed on making every area of our community as safe as possible, even those areas that are not fashionable to talk about. Education is the key to achieving this.

But now we are going to take a step further into the darkness and discover how terrible some fractious elements of chemsex culture can be. We're going to east London, to an area called Barking, and an apartment on Cooke Street. The apartment is the home of Stephen Port, who in 2016 was sentenced to life imprisonment after he horrifically raped and murdered four young gay men.

7

THE CASE OF
STEPHEN PORT

This chapter could be titled a number of things: 'The sham-bolic police handling of a rampant gay serial killer' or 'The beautiful lives lost of Anthony Walgate, Gabriel Kovari, Daniel Whitworth and Jack Taylor'. It could focus on how, in 2014 and 2015, a cunning and determined man in east London managed to rape and kill four young men without the police becoming suspicious or noticing what now seem such obvious trends. The entire story, which at the time of writing has still not come to its terrifying and sickening end – a further fifty-eight deaths are being re-examined following Port's sentencing on 25 November 2016 at the Old Bailey – would probably be thrown in the bin if a screenwriter ever pitched it to a Hollywood studio.

Simply put, it's unbelievable.

Port's four victims all had different upbringings, and they all had futures ahead of them, all as beautifully diverse as the experiences and personalities that had made each of them unique individuals. But the victims met their tragic ends in almost identical circumstances, and all because of one sick human being.

Anthony Walgate was twenty-three, originally from Hull, and lived in London, where he was studying the subject that was his major passion in life: fashion. He was brought up in a loving family in the Foredyke Avenue area of east Hull. His parents, Sarah and Tom, were separated and later divorced. Having studied hard at David Lister School and then at Hull College, Anthony earned a place at the University of Middlesex to study art, fashion and design. He was just coming to the end of his second year at the university when he was brutally murdered. Like so many young people, Anthony had found London, his academic studies and the cost of living to be a challenge. To earn extra money to get by in the capital, he joined the escort website Sleepyboys. It was on this site that he was initially contacted by Port.

Gabriel Kovari was born in Slovakia. He left his home country at a young age to establish better opportunities for himself. According to *The Guardian*, he had felt that Slovakia was 'too conservative and intolerant'. Gabriel came to the UK to find a community he would feel safe in. He was twenty-two when Port murdered him.

Daniel Whitworth grew up in Gravesend, Kent, attending Dartford Grammar School as a teenager. He was in a long-term relationship with his partner, Ricky Waumsley, and worked as a chef in London's financial centre. He was an active, outdoors-type of guy; his last tweet is a picture of him enjoying an apple in an orchard, which he cheekily captioned 'taking a bag home ;) #freshisbest'. His Twitter profile highlights his zest for life and the pride he had for the person he was turning into. Daniel was only twenty-one when Stephen Port killed him.

Jack Taylor, twenty-five, was a forklift truck driver who lived with his parents in Dagenham, Essex, just four miles from where he would meet his tragic and brutal end. Like a lot of people, Jack preferred to keep his sexuality private, but he did access some parts of the LGBT community via apps like Grindr. It was on Grindr that Jack met Port, and then made late-night arrangements to travel to Barking to hook up.

Jack was the serial killer's last victim.

Port's killing spree had started with him reaching out to Anthony Walgate via the Sleepyboys website on 17 June 2014. Port offered 23-year-old Anthony £800 to travel to his east London home on Cooke Street. Later that day, Anthony travelled to Barking station, where he was met by Port, who took him to his apartment. At some point during the following twenty-four hours, Port administered a lethal dose of G to Anthony, before raping him while he was unconscious and then dumping his dead body outside his flat. Port reported the death to the police just before 8 a.m. on the morning of 19 June without initially giving them his name. He claimed that a boy had 'collapsed, had a seizure or was drunk' outside the apartment. Later, the police began to notice inaccuracies in Port's version of events and became suspicious. However, they later accepted Port's changed story: that the pair had had sex, but that Anthony had taken an overdose of drugs and become unconscious.

Incredibly, the investigating officers didn't view Port as a key suspect in Anthony's death; instead, they concentrated on charging him with perverting the course of justice for lying to the police. In March 2015, Port was convicted of the charge and jailed for eight months. He served just three. But before his spell behind bars he raped and murdered two other men, and then killed a fourth soon after his release. Anthony's parents later criticised the Metropolitan Police for not keeping them informed of Port's actions and for their failure to prevent the subsequent murders.

Port's second victim was Gabriel Kovari. His body was found propped up against the wall in a graveyard near Cooke Street by 65-year-old dog walker Barbara Denham in the early hours of 22 August. Barbara Denham later described how she found Gabriel: 'Because there was no movement, nothing, I decided to turn back, to try and get his attention. I just touched him on the ankle, he just felt cold to the touch.'

The discovery of Gabriel's body came just nine weeks after Anthony's murder.

Gabriel, who had been couch-surfing in Port's living room, was drugged and raped. His body was then dumped in the graveyard 400 metres from Port's flat. But even though the graveyard was just a short distance away from Port's home, and despite the fact that it was barely two months since the discovery of Anthony Walgate's body, the police did not suspect any foul play.

In an eerie twist, the body of the third victim, young chef Daniel Whitworth, was also found by Barbara Denham, the same dog walker who three weeks earlier had discovered the remains of Gabriel Kovari. 'Oh please,' she would say at the trial when describing the scene, 'let that be somebody asleep – it cannot be the same thing again, in exactly the same place.'

When Daniel's body was discovered, detectives found a 'suicide note' in which the 21-year-old 'confessed' that he had killed Gabriel Kovari by accident and was committing suicide as he could no longer live with the guilt. The letter ended, 'BTW please do not blame the guy I was with last night, we only had sex and then I left, he knows nothing of what I have done.' Daniel had not written this note, of course. By planting the note, Port managed to throw detectives off the scent. The police left him alone.

This is the full version of the 'suicide note' found in the pocket of Daniel Whitworth.

I am sorry to everyone, mainly my family, but I can't go on anymore, I took the life of my friend Gabriel Kline, we was just having some fun at a mate's place and I got carried away and gave him another shot of G. I didn't notice while we was [sic] having sex that he had stopped breathing. I tried everything to get him to breathe again but it was too late, it was an accident, but I blame myself for what happened and I didn't tell my family I went out. I know I would go to prison if I go to the police and I can't do that to my family and at least this way I can at least be with Gabriel again, I hope he will forgive me.

BTW Please do not blame the guy I was with last night, we only had sex then I left, he knows nothing of what I have done. I have taken what g I have left with sleeping pills so if it does kill me it's what I deserve. Feeling dizey [*sic*] now as took 10 min ago so hoping you understand my writing. I dropped my phone on way here so it should be in the grass somewhere. Sorry to everyone.

Love always Daniel P W.

Some time passed between the discovery of Daniel's body and that of the fourth victim, 25-year-old Jack Taylor, because Port had been jailed for perverting the course of justice in connection with Anthony Walgate's murder. Port was jailed for eight months, but was released with an electronic tag on 4 June after serving twelve weeks behind bars. He killed for the last time three months after being released.

By this time, a friend of Gabriel Kovari had become more than just suspicious. John Pape had been hosting Gabriel in his spare room for some time before Gabriel had decided to move out and sofa-surf at Port's flat. John later told the BBC:

At the time I was thinking, you've got now three young men turning up dead in the same area in Barking. There's something very wrong going on here. And because I knew Gabriel, I started to worry that I might be in danger. So I called the detective from Barking and Dagenham and I said, 'If this is murder you have to tell me because I am concerned for my own safety.' I was assured that it wasn't murder.

For various reasons, Port's fourth and final victim, Jack Taylor, did not openly discuss his sexuality. He was a private person who didn't frequent the gay scene typically; his encounters were somewhat restricted to hook-up apps.

CCTV later showed Jack walking with Port to the killer's home at around 3 a.m. on Sunday 13 September. A short while later, Jack was drugged with G, and as he began to slip into unconsciousness, Port raped him. When Jack was dead, Port did as he had done with two of his previous victims: he took Jack's body to St Margaret's graveyard and dumped it there. Unfathomably, the police still refused to suspect foul play or to establish a link between the four deaths, even though three of the men's bodies had been found in the same place. Jack's two older sisters decided to take the matter into their own hands and began their own investigation. The actions of Donna and Jenny Taylor would force the police into reviewing the previous three deaths and result in the arrest of Jack's killer, Stephen Port.

Astonishingly, the CCTV footage that showed Stephen Port walking alongside Jack through the streets of Barking had never been viewed by police; they only became aware of the footage when Donna and Jenny, through their own detective work, viewed it and then passed it on to a local newspaper. When the newspaper ran the story, the police were forced to act and Stephen Port was finally arrested. He will never experience freedom again.

It would be revealed at the trial that, after killing Gabriel in his Barking flat, Port called his sister, Sharon, to tell her there was a body in his bed. She advised him to go to the police and explain what she thought were the innocent circumstances surrounding the situation. Instead, Port dumped Gabriel's body in the graveyard.

Wickedly, he then logged onto Facebook and for weeks tormented Gabriel's grieving ex-boyfriend Thierry: Port pretended to be an American and claimed Gabriel had attended a sex party with someone called Dan on the night he was murdered. Dan, of course, was Port's third victim, Daniel Whitworth. Port was, as summarised by Stephen Rees QC, prosecuting, 'laying the groundwork' to implicate Daniel over the murder and attempting further to distance himself from any possibility of being associated with it, or those before it.

Port's horrific crimes are not limited to the murders of these four boys. He was also convicted of raping a further seven men and, ultimately, was found guilty of eleven counts of rape or sexual assault and four counts of murder. As already mentioned, a further fifty-eight deaths are being reviewed, and it is possible that Port will face further charges and new trials. But all that put aside, the question remains: how could he possibly have been allowed to carry out these horrendous crimes, when a huge number of clues were screaming out at law enforcement officers? If not outright idiocy, can we suspect that institutionalised homophobia lies behind the total lack of action by the police in east London? This is something many people have suggested, including veteran campaigner Peter Tatchell.

A generous interpretation might be that the officers involved thought that this was a chemsex party gone wrong, and that no ill intention was involved. They may have thought that gay men have engaged in some recreational drug use, and this turned into a terrible tragedy, on four occasions. Perhaps there could have even been an element of 'we don't want to be seen to be intruding or harassing the LGBT community'. Some officers may have felt that going in hard on this might damage relations with the LGBT community. There are lots of possibilities, but at the end of the day the evidence doesn't support that kind of generous interpretation.

Even if the deaths were the result of chemsex parties gone wrong, to not report the deaths to the police, and to dump the bodies in a public place, is a criminal offence. Why didn't they therefore ask themselves the question why, in three of these circumstances, did nobody call the police; why didn't anybody phone an ambulance? So I don't buy the generous interpretation. I think there must have been, at the very least, incompetence or homophobia involved. If this is confirmed, the officers involved should face disciplinary action.

If the police's underlying homophobia did lead to the preventable deaths of three more young men, following the discovery of Anthony Walgate's body on 19 June 2014, then it's fair to add this to my earlier concerns about how the police treat gay men who have been sexually assaulted while under the influence of drugs.

Would a better investigation at that early point have prevented the killing and rape of others? This book says yes. If the police had been more suspicious about why Port lied about discovering Anthony's body, or if they had searched his mobile phone and computer, they would have discovered how Anthony was lured to Port's apartment by the promise of financial reward. Just this simple piece of detective work could have potentially prevented Gabriel's, Daniel's and Jack's deaths. If the police had searched Port's flat, they might have found drug paraphernalia, perhaps even traces of G – the drug Port used to kill Anthony. This would have waved red flags right in the face of the Metropolitan Police. But they failed to follow up on any hints of foul play. The police failed the parents of Anthony Walgate. They failed the three other victims who were brutally murdered by Stephen Port. And, once again, they failed London's gay community.

In October 2015, and following the arrest of Stephen Port, the Metropolitan Police referred themselves to the IPCC (Independent Police Complaints Commission), which led to seven officers facing the most serious charge of gross misconduct, and a further ten facing the lesser charge of misconduct. The charges, which affect officers in ranks ranging from constable to inspector, relate to how the force responded to the deaths before any investigation was launched and include specific criticisms about how evidence was examined and how the similarities between each of the victims were not considered. Those facing gross misconduct charges could be sacked if they are found guilty. When Port's guilty verdicts were returned, Metropolitan Police Commander Stuart Cundy wrote to the victims' families offering his condolences and apologising for the force's handling of the case. For the grieving families, though, this wasn't enough.

Our small family has had to endure unspeakable grief at various stages coming to terms and having to face up to some of the terrible turn of events in the space of two years. It's difficult, to say the least. Daniel has had a significant impact on our lives; they will never be the same again. We are emotionally and physically exhausted.

Today has marked the end of a large part of our battle; Stephen Port has been found guilty of murder, and we are one step closer to making sure he will never be able to put another family through this again.

As for our boy Daniel, we feel unable to comment any more at this time. Suffice to say, we are bereft at the loss of such a clever, talented and much-loved boy, and we are yet to concentrate on other areas of the accountability; the fight goes on until all our questions are answered.

– Mandy Pearson, Daniel Whitworth's stepmum.

We have just come out of court and got justice for our Jack. We can now let Jack rest in peace. Jack was a loving son, a brother, uncle and grandson, a brother-in-law and nephew and a true inspiration to everyone who knew him. He was the life and soul of our family; our lives will never be the same. And we would like to thank you all for showing an interest in our Jack because he meant the world to us.

– Jenny and Donna Taylor, sisters of Jack Taylor.

Anthony, Gabriel, Daniel and Jack ... rest in peace.

It would be unfair to not mention another key element concerning the way in which Port was able to select his victims and kill them. It's impossible not to draw attention to something that keeps cropping up as we continue to explore what chemsex is and why it has boomed. I'm talking again about hook-up apps and technology, and how these played a part in the Stephen Port story. Without such key technological ingredients, Port would never have been able to lure three of his victims to their tragic deaths. It poses the question: why isn't our virtual gay community policed better? In fact, why isn't it policed at all?

Two weeks before Port was convicted of his brutal crimes, another high-profile murder trial grabbed the headlines. It focused on Stefano Brizzi, who was accused of murdering police officer Gordon Semple. Gordon's death held my attention, possibly more so than normal, because I knew him as we both used to drink at the same pub in central London.

Some months earlier, Brizzi and Semple had exchanged messages over Grindr; things had progressed and they decided to meet. Gordon was invited to Brizzi's Southwark apartment on the Peabody estate, a short walk from the Tate Modern, and the pair then engaged in intercourse. At the beginning of the trial, the prosecuting QC told jury members that they would require 'broad minds and strong stomachs'. It was said that PC Gordon Semple, although in a relationship at the time of his death, had been 'promiscuous' and, as the *Daily Telegraph* would later report, had used Grindr for 'extreme' sexual liaisons. Gordon's killer was said to have been obsessed with *Breaking Bad*. In an episode in the first series, Walter White, one of the show's main characters, kills a rival drug pusher and dissolves the body in a bathtub of acid. Brizzi, the jury would hear, attempted to dispose of Gordon Semple's body in the same manner. After strangling Gordon during 'extreme' sex, Brizzi went to a hardware shop, where he was captured on CCTV buying acid. He dismembered Gordon's body and hoped the pieces would vanish. It was only after the smell became so awful that neighbours in the estate grew suspicious and alerted the police. When the police arrived, Brizzi confessed to killing Gordon, telling officers: 'I have tried to dissolve the body ... I have killed a police officer. I met him on Grindr and I killed him. Satan told me to.'

This is the stuff of nightmares. I can't even roughly guess how many strangers' flats I have gone to, without first telling anyone of my whereabouts, generally unprepared should something go wrong. Gordon was a giant of a man, and a copper at that: police officers know how to look after themselves. Yet Brizzi was able to manipulate his victim, and seemingly with ease: if it can happen to Gordon, it can happen to any of us. But even as I say this, I know that I still haven't really ever considered what to do if something doesn't feel right – if something goes wrong.

• • •

When I went on Grindr's website in January 2017, it was as sexy as you would expect. In fact, if I hadn't already had the app on my phone, a visit to the website would have made me want to download it. It was slick. Running along the top of the homepage were a number of options, and the word 'Values' caught my eyes.

'We strive to create a safe space where all are welcome to be who they are and express themselves without fear of judgment.'

Did you notice the word 'strive'?

Now let's see what Grindr says about drugs.

'We do not condone the abuse of drugs and those who use our platform for the use of sales and distribution of them. Keeping our grid drug-free is a top priority.'

How? What has Grindr actively done to prevent drug distribution through the use of the app? I can turn my phone on at any time of the day and either see someone offering drugs via their profile information – seemingly without a worry in the world – or be actively approached by someone fancying their chances of a quick sale. Is Grindr serious about tackling all of this? And if so, what resources is it committing to the fight? Grindr has explicitly highlighted tackling drugs as being a top priority, but I'm just not convinced.

Below the section on drugs, there was a paragraph on prostitution, which again didn't go into too much detail on how the matter was policed, and then there was a bit about discrimination. But right at the bottom of the page there was a call to action for you, the user:

Let's work together to make these values a part of everybody's experience on Grindr. We encourage you to take action whenever you see any of the negative behaviour described above. Report what you see, flag profiles, and speak up. And make sure to do it thoughtfully. Let's do our part to make Grindr a better community now and for years to come.

Suddenly, after the few sentences on Grindr's own commitment to tackling a few issues like drugs, rent boys and racism, the ball is played back to our side of the court and it feels like the onus is suddenly more focused on us: if you see it, report it. Is this what Grindr bases its enforcement policy on – the reporting of misdeeds by those users who only want to use the service ethically? I contacted Grindr in search of answers to some of my questions, but I never received a reply. Grindr has since redesigned its website and the 'Values' page no longer exists; the closest thing I can find is a 'Profile Guidelines' page, but this has no mention of drugs.

Are we wrong to expect that businesses operate ethically? We are all human and have to take responsibility for all other aspects of our lives. Let's face it, in the court cases that have been discussed in this chapter, Grindr was not brought to trial, or even heavily criticised for the role it played in allowing Stephen Port to connect with his victims. But are we guilty here of trying to instil a moral code on a commercial business? Can we blame an app that is designed with the intention of making as much money as possible for its shareholders? Peter Tatchell believes that more should be done to create a safe environment for app users, but he also lays some of the blame on us, the gay community.

'I'm surprised that LGBT press and LGBT organisations have not – in the wake of the Port murder trial – done more in educating people about safe dating. That seems like a big failure on the community's behalf,' Tatchell says.

If giants like Grindr are only going to put up a user safety page of less than 500 words on their sites, signed off with a call for users to report any wrongdoing, then perhaps we need to take this one on our shoulders as a community; this is our responsibility. We can't force hook-up apps to better police their environments, but we can – all of us – learn how to use these hook-up apps more safely. Perhaps our community leaders, such as the likes of Stonewall, should be taking this on.

Peter Tatchell explains:

The obvious advice is to warn people that if they're meeting a new date, the RV should always be in a visible public place. Beforehand, they should make sure they get the number of the person, and phone to check that it is their number. Then before they go to the date they should alert someone they trust that they're meeting up – when and where – and give the name and number of the person they're meeting. Perhaps, as an added precaution, they should indicate to the person they're meeting that they've taken these steps. If those steps are followed, the chances of being raped or killed are significantly slashed.

Neither Peter Tatchell nor I are calling for Grindr or Scruff, or any of the other apps, to come down heavy on their users and infringe on privacy; let's face it, we've all sent images via apps that we don't want it to be open season for anybody to look at. But maybe, just maybe, apps and sites could do more than they currently do to make sure that everyone, with just a few taps of their iPhones, can get access to tips like those that Peter gave to me.

Perhaps we could all spend a little more time looking out for each other, too: we don't want our younger gay brothers to wander off into the wilderness underprepared and possibly into danger. There are four sets of parents whose sons' lives came to a tragic end in east London not so long ago: parents who I'm sure would want us to do all we can to prevent lightning from striking again. We've locked up Port and thrown away the key. And on Sunday 5 February 2017, Brizzi decided to end his own life in his prison cell, perhaps unable to live with himself and the crime he had committed. But there are other monsters still out there, searching for future victims and looking to harm people. And, as we are about to learn, it's not always by way of rape or murder.

8

WHAT WOULD
THE *DAILY MAIL* SAY?

Calvin is a 34-year-old mixed-race man living in south London with his partner, and I've returned to talk to him about his personal journey, and to get his thoughts on how his life was put on hold by a chemsex addiction.

On the face of it, Calvin has everything he needs in life: caring lover, steady job, youthful good looks and an air of confidence that shouts 'sorted'. He's sitting at a table which he's reserved in one of the many pretty cafes dotted around Soho, and stands up to greet me when I arrive. He shakes my hand, moves in to give me a hug and I affectionately peck him once on each cheek. All very standard: I've known Calvin for about six years. But beneath his familiar face lies something else: a past, a struggle, a dark story that when it's told will reduce me to tears.

Our coffees are brought over: I choose a slice of cake and he does the same. But a short while later, when there's no longer anything else to keep us from doing so, we have to confront the reason we are both sitting here. Calvin, like so many of us, is good at masking his issues: all gay men are good at this, right? Like so many others, he can pull out that smile, make those around him feel at ease, and is genuinely warm and caring. But there's a problem.

Calvin is recovering; he has been for a couple of years. But during the peak of his addiction to chemsex he was slamming crystal meth into his arm, thighs and feet for up to five days straight at a time. As we chat, I start to see behind those eyes. Calvin stares long into the distance, and occasionally falls silent while his mind takes him back to a terrible memory, something that still weighs heavily on his shoulders. It's difficult for him to keep his mask on as I ask certain questions, and when the mask slips, or when he takes it off for just a second, the bright young confident man is gone and you glimpse the shattered soul of a man in pain.

'Eleven this winter,' he tells me, referring to how many drug-related deaths he's aware of: gay men at chill-outs, chemsex parties or even at home alone. Eleven! He asks me if I knew such-and-such – 'Oh, you must know him, or at least his friend; he went on Christmas Eve' – and I do vaguely recall the person. We then spend a minute talking about the mutual friends we have lost: Robin a few years back, Daven just last autumn. It's an excruciatingly sad few moments, and we're united in grief at the loss of these beautiful human beings. I ask Calvin how many acquaintances he's lost over the last five years; his response is jaw-dropping.

I know Calvin's story inside out. He's been very generous and has been open with his memories, thoughts and accounts of surrendering almost his entire life to drugs and sex. He's been homeless and he's been attacked – sometimes horrifically. He's been sectioned and he's tried to kill himself. He's also been diagnosed as HIV-positive.

'I know someone purposely gave me this. It was set up to happen. I was given too much, my senses were completely shot, and the guy put me in his sling and came inside me. I got HIV,' he says.

Calvin's experiences are not limited to just these; he's got so many other scars and painful memories that it's difficult to pick which stories to relay. They're all relevant and his account of the two-and-a-half years he spent in the chemsex world is much darker than my own story, and that of others I've engaged with. It's terrifying to think that what happened to Calvin could easily have happened to me and to so many others. And more terrifying still, this is happening to people right now.

Calvin drinks from his cup then leans closer; he wants to talk more quietly.

At the start, and definitely after my break-up, I became hooked on porn. I was watching it constantly, and it didn't make me happy; the opposite, actually. Every time I watched porn it made me depressed. When I got depressed I wanted some drugs to make me happy again. These two factors each started feeding on each other. Drugs would make me horny, porn would make me sad.

Calvin stops abruptly and looks over my shoulder towards the entrance of the café – Patisserie Valerie on Old Compton Street

– and it seems as if he's suddenly spotted someone. There's a look of concern on his face and then, in an instant, he's back. I look over and can't see anybody, so I think nothing more of it.

Then one night someone offered me a smoke of his crystal meth pipe; that was a real turning point for me. That's when it changed: I went from being a bit of an occasional dabbler to full-on planning my life around Tina. This is when I abandoned my life as I knew it, and began pushing the sexual limits I was prepared to allow myself to explore. These chems, they don't just reduce your inhibitions, they actually take them away altogether.

And then, about two days into a party one time, a couple of guys turned up, older chaps, quite bear-like, and they were doing something different. They were injecting themselves with the drugs the rest of us were snorting or drinking, to get an even bigger kick. I was so high as it was, I said 'fine'. I've never had a fear of needles; they didn't seem like a big issue. But I wasn't at all prepared for the euphoric feeling; the rush of blood to my head and the state of complete ecstasy 'slamming' would give me. At this stage my life was already screwed, it couldn't possibly have got any worse, or so I thought.

Calvin tells me his habit of slamming at sex parties went on for about two-and-a-half years. He became a regular at people's apartments across London; indeed, he recalls occasions to me that feature Camden, Hackney, Clapham and Tooting. He's circumnavigated the chemsex globe. But something Calvin wasn't prepared for was the mental health side effects that go hand in hand with slamming crystal meth into your veins, and which would eventually see him sectioned under the Mental Health Act.

I scaled London west to east one day; I just walked. I didn't even realise my mind was elsewhere. I was convinced someone was following me. I hid in toilets, criss-crossed roads trying to shake off the tail behind me, but there wasn't anyone there; it was all in my head. It was two days after I'd slammed more Tina than I should have and I literally lost my mind. I was so scared I wanted to die.

Paranoia, as we saw earlier, is a major side effect not just of Tina, but of mephedrone too. From my own experiences of sniffing meph, I know that hours, even days, later, the expectation that something terrible in your life is about to happen is a very real worry. The first time this really struck me was in my apartment. The family who live upstairs are somewhat heavy-footed, and when not on a paranoia-filled comedown, I was used to them traipsing up and down. But one time, after a heavy weekend, every time they made just the slightest noise, my heart skipped a beat and I couldn't control the panic.

There was also the time my flatmate had to slap me around the face and tell me my Twitter account had not been hacked into by the Russian government, who I swore blind were working in unison with the *Daily Mail* to expose me as a drug user. It might be amusing to recall all this now, but at that precise moment, the fear that gripped my chest was extremely upsetting. Calvin agrees wholeheartedly when I tell him this.

'I was convinced the BBC were on my doorstep: I've believed the police had planted a listening device in my kitchen. I've thought things that normal people would think utterly bonkers, but when the psychosis sets in, it's real,' Calvin says.

In the summer of 2016, Calvin suffered his worst relapse.

'I thought this time would be it. I now think the next time I have a mishap, if it's as large as this last one, they'll probably find me dead.'

This causes me to panic. I touch his arm and tell him to call me any time he needs help. He thanks me, and offers the same assistance should I ever need it. We both sip our coffees.

Calvin tells me the story of his latest relapse. It starts with him feeling down. Something he can't quite put his finger on made him buy drugs. Once high, he drifted on to some apps.

'Grindr is just the tip of the iceberg. Have you heard of NKP?' Calvin asks.

I shake my head.

'Nasty Kink Pigs,' Calvin explains.

It's an anything goes, no holds barred playground for pushing the sexual limits. I downloaded the app, started a chat with someone not too far away. He came over. The plan was for us to slam together. By now I had obviously completely fallen off the wagon. When this happens, I can't stop.

The guy travelled over to Calvin's apartment, things progressed and the pair began to have sex. As arranged, needles were made up and the visitor offered to inject Calvin with Tina. The man injected him. Seconds later, it hit his brain. Calvin was muted by the immediate effect. But even in his incapacitated state, he realised something was wrong.

He'd administered too much. He'd overdosed on what he told me he'd prepared. It was bad. I managed to push him away, and saw that he'd made up another needle which he was going to give me too. He was trying to either render me unconscious, or maybe even kill me. Within seconds he made his excuses and left.

Just the one needle was enough, though. I found myself the following day suffering the worst paranoia I have ever felt. I wanted to kill myself, and I was ready to.

Calvin was sectioned after his partner took him to hospital. He was diagnosed with acute psychosis. Calvin shakes his head as he ends his account of August's problems,

'That other needle would have killed me, or at least, the increased effect on my mental well-being might have been enough to tip me over the brink and do it myself.'

At this point I think back to how frequently I saw or heard from Calvin during the period all this happened. He had disappeared. I had been none the wiser, but my friend had been enduring the most unthinkable agony, and had been sectioned for his own well-being. It made me think about who I had reached out to in the past when I'd needed help and I wondered who I could turn to if I ever found myself in the same situation as Calvin. Bar my best friend, I realised that I had been bottling up all the bad times and that I had reached out to hardly anybody.

I subscribe to the theory made by others – perhaps most notably in the recent book *Straight Jacket* by Matthew Todd – that this keeping of things hidden, this wearing of a mask, is all part and parcel of us having been secretly gay for some period of our lives. For me, that secret period lasted from the age of about thirteen until I finally came out at the age of eighteen; for others it can be a much longer period. My formative years were a time when I pretended to be something I wasn't, and as a result of what happened during those years I still wear a mask when I need to, because for me it's easier.

I'm keen to learn more about Calvin, and specifically about the time when he became HIV-positive. He tells me:

Out of nowhere, I suddenly suffered three weeks of cold sweats and high temperatures. I was encouraged by colleagues at work to take the day off work, and a few specifically told me to take a HIV test. I went to Mortimer Market clinic with the guy I was sort of seeing, but once I had the result he left me there to deal with the consequences. To be honest, I was relieved and didn't really get upset about the diagnosis. I remember leaving alone, and started to text friends and to be honest they were more upset than I was. I got home and relayed the information to my then flatmate/boyfriend, who wasn't surprised but wasn't angry or cross.

'Did it make you reassess the activities you were putting yourself into?' I ask.

'No, quite the opposite,' Calvin replies. 'I wanted to play with other HIV-positive men, and I was always honest about my status. And I became undetectable quickly. I needed that emotional connection chemsex gave, something I couldn't get when sober. Chemsex allowed me to be uninhibited, which I needed.'

Some might question why Calvin receiving life-changing information like becoming HIV-positive didn't act as a turning point to putting his life on track.

'It doesn't work like that though, does it?' he says. 'Once I was positive, I thought, well, fuck it, I've got it now, I might as well continue with it. On the surface I didn't let my changing status bother me too much, the drugs definitely masked that, but niggling away in my head was the realisation that this is something I was going to live with for the rest of my days.'

Since the emergence of PrEP, a daily course of medication that when followed correctly can reduce your chances of contracting HIV by up to 90 per cent (one study in the United States placed it as being 100 per cent effective), people who attend chemsex parties and who take risks with their sexual health now have a new weapon in their arsenal with which they can protect themselves. And, of course, it makes perfect sense to go on the medication if you do sometimes lose the ability to think straight, as it were, at chemsex parties, or if your inhibitions are lowered to such an extent that you are oblivious to the risks of letting a stranger have sex with you bareback.

But some view this silver bullet against HIV negatively, and there have been claims, even from within the gay community itself, that people will use the medication as a green light to do anything they like with respect to their sexual health. This is an issue that I discussed with Greg Owen. Greg, whom we met earlier, is the most prominent campaigner for PrEP in the UK and says:

If PrEP had been available thirty years ago, when our community, our friends, our lovers and our brothers and sisters were literally dropping dead around us in a painful and tortuous fashion, then our community would have jumped on it, celebrated it and welcomed it with open arms. I'm certain nobody would have opposed it. It is fantastic that we have made such huge and revolutionary advances recently in the treatment options available for those of us living with HIV. If we are fortunate enough to live in an area where we can access free or affordable healthcare, we can expect to live a full and healthy life. This is to be celebrated too, but our brothers and sisters before us did not die of AIDS so that we could become complacent with HIV and allow ourselves to be immersed in AIDS apathy. It started with them; it can end with us. We have the tools to stop and end HIV and AIDS. We need to use them. We can't allow our privileges to diminish our responsibilities in this global healthcare issue.

On Facebook, a group called Gay Men Against PrEP – made up of our own community members – lobbies against the medication. The general tone of the group's Facebook page is aggressive, with their overall argument trending towards the idea that gay men should simply use condoms, that PrEP is a burden on taxpayers, and will cause an unprecedented increase in STI transmissions as the medication can only reduce the risk of the singular condition of HIV. I would love to be able to say that a spokesperson came forward from the group to argue their case in detail, but no one would. They were immediately on the defensive and, it has to be said, became outright *offensive* when I approached them and explained that a leading PrEP campaigner had also spoken to me about the medication. This was the group's response:

'Prominent prep campaigner? U [*sic*] mean the chemsex bareback addict who has been sectioned for his mental health issues? Interviewing them reveals your slant. That his opinions are somehow valid.'

I decided that engaging with this group was probably not going to be fruitful, and I also felt they were incredibly vicious in how they presented what could have been a considered argument.

And it *is* a considered argument. Many friends, some of them high-profile, have told me that they disagree with the rollout of PrEP for anybody who wants it. But, and this is interesting, it is impossible to get any of them to give their names and talk on the record about their opposition to the medication.

Matthew Hodson, formally CEO of GMFA but today the person behind Aidsmap, told me that he felt the opposition was short-sighted.

I've always believed the way to treat HIV is to have a combination approach. We need to recognise that a single approach to prevention isn't going to work. It's clear that condom use as a strategy does not work for some people. If my job is to prevent HIV infections, my job is to promote that whichever way I can. When PrEP came along, I thought, 'Here is a tool that's going to work for people who aren't going to use condoms consistently.'

One reason many people oppose PrEP is the lack of protection it provides against other STIs and diseases, things like hep C and syphilis. Some say it might even add to the problems these other infections bring. In response, Matthew told me he felt there was a necessity to become 'creative' in looking at ways of tackling this possibility.

If we want to end HIV, PrEP is a tool we have to use. If we want to end incidents of other STIs, we are going to have to think creatively about how we educate people to use condoms and having less sexual partners, about having sexual delay. The urge to have sex is primal ... men are more socialised to this, but you see girls drunk on a Saturday night too; drink is part of sexual liberation. It's a larger picture than the simplistic approach that PrEP fixes HIV, and that other STIs will flourish.

After a successful trial in the UK, NHS England, following a period of reflection, believed that PrEP should not be rolled out across the board for gay men, MSM (men who have sex with men) and other groups at a high risk of contracting HIV (defined as sex workers, those in relationships where one partner is HIV-positive, people who slam and those who won't use condoms). This triggered different reactions from people like Greg, who had campaigned for it to be widely available, and groups like Gay Men Against PrEP who opposed the medication being made available for free. Opponents of the drug found themselves supported by many national newspapers using questionable language and, in one or two cases, all-out homophobia directed against those the drug would help.

'My initial reaction was "WHAT THE FUCK!"' Greg says. 'When Jeremy Hunt was pushed by Professor Sheena McCormack over providing PrEP, his immediate reaction was: "I can't possibly commission THAT. What would the *Daily Mail* say?"'

'So was the decision based on bigotry?' I ask Greg.

'If this was a health condition that disproportionately affected cis-born, straight, white, middle-aged men, we wouldn't even be having this conversation,' Greg replies. 'They'd be tripping over themselves to look after themselves: just like they do with statins, diabetes and Viagra. Instead, they pitted PrEP and the "irresponsible dirty promiscuous gays" against kids with cystic fibrosis. Fucking scandalous!'

I find it impossible to disagree with Greg Owen on this.

The National AIDS Trust, the UK's leading HIV and AIDS

advocacy organisation, mounted a legal challenge in the High Court against NHS England's decision – and won. The *Daily Mail* spun the story by pitching those PrEP is primarily aimed at helping against groups including sick children, which had been effective in turning the wider population against a universal distribution of PrEP. According to the newspaper:

> The legal decision is of wider importance because of its potential impact on the provision of other services, including hearing implants for children with deficient or missing auditory nerves, prosthetics for lower limb loss, and a drug for treating certain mutations in children aged two to five with cystic fibrosis.
>
> Nine new treatments and services that NHS England had planned to make available to patients were put on hold pending the court's ruling.

The *Daily Mail* was not alone in reporting the High Court ruling with stigma-inducing undertones. Inflammatory language was, for a couple of days, commonplace in the British press, and commentators like the odious Katie Hopkins had their say by making sweeping generalisations.

In response to the High Court ruling, which was of course appealed, NHS England issued a press release that was heavily criticised for how it worded the NHS position. It started by saying: 'PrEP is a measure to prevent HIV transmission, particularly for men who have high-risk condomless sex with multiple male partners.' It ended by confirming that the NHS would continue to fight against handing out PrEP to those who need it most. It looked and felt like NHS England – completely public funded – was making a moral judgement on the activities of some within the wider LGBT community. This is not what we expect from a taxpayer-funded organisation. But the National AIDS Trust did win in the High Court, and it looks like PrEP will very soon be available for free on the NHS. Wherever you sit in relation to the argument, this cannot be described as anything other than progress. It will prevent HIV.

I was particularly pleased by the eventual outcome in the High Court, as the options available to those who needed PrEP had meant vulnerable groups who might require it most were the least likely to get it. Unless you were on a trial programme, you could only get your hands on PrEP privately. I have criticised 56 Dean Street before for privately selling PrEP. But I have since learned that Dean Street was actually selling these tablets at cost price: it was not profiting from selling the drug in any sense. My research found that it costs around £500 to get going on PrEP when bought from a private medical practice. But now, thanks to Greg, there is another option.

Greg Owen co-founded the revolutionary website iWant-PrEPnow.co.uk, which, together with his excellent PrEP and HIV-awareness work mentioned earlier, has been hugely responsible for getting PrEP to thousands of people who need it most. The website acts as a signpost to online shopping locations where PrEP is available on the open market. Once bought, it's delivered to your front door typically at about the £40-per-month mark. In 2016 alone, Greg's website directed 44,000 people in London to safe places where PrEP can be bought, and in turn, where preventative treatment can be started. The knock-on effect of all this? There was a 40 per cent drop in new infection rates in London last year. There's nothing further to say about the justification of PrEP and its immediate roll-out here.

Public Health England's 2016 announcement that the number of gay men with HIV in London had hit an all-time high of one in seven, while, as we've just discovered, a number of leading sexual health clinics report a 40 per cent drop in new infections, suggests there are two different worlds out there. But the reason for the contrasting pictures may be quite straightforward, says Aidsmap's Matthew Hodson.

You have more people living longer with HIV than ever before. In the '80s and '90s, if you became HIV-positive, you quite likely died. With the monumental leaps forward in antiviral treatment of the last twenty or so years, today if you are diagnosed HIV-positive, you're likely going to have a normal life expectancy, just like non-HIV-positive people.

Matthew went on to explain that the reductions seen in London, specifically at the Dean Street clinic, which has a majority gay and bisexual client base, are probably due to the impact of PrEP, even though it has not yet been rolled out universally and for free.

Think of the patient-zero theory. If you can get PrEP to the people who are attending chemsex parties and having unprotected sex with sometimes seven or eight people, if that person goes on PrEP, you are potentially preventing the passing on of HIV to seven or eight other people. The drop in new infections supports the idea that the people who are responsible for passing their infection on or who might be majority responsible for passing it on, getting those people on PrEP, well, you can see how it reduces the numbers affected.

Matthew's reasoning about the sudden drop in new infections stands up to criticism. Those who have recently contracted HIV and who are unaware that they are HIV-positive are most likely to transmit the infection. However, once they begin treatment, their viral load will drop and this also greatly decreases the chances of the infection being passed on.

If I was unaware that I'd recently contracted HIV, and I then hosted or attended a sex party where drug use was central to the fun and pleasure, unprotected sex might occur. Because my viral load (how much HIV is in my blood) is off the scale, I might pass the condition to those I had sex with. But if the guys I had sex with were on PrEP – this wonder drug that has to be taken just once a day – they would have a safety net. And this is what Matthew Hodson thinks is happening now. People have essentially taken responsibility for their own HIV futures in a way that they haven't done with condoms for decades. PrEP works.

Once people are aware of their status, most of them will begin treatment immediately; that's the advice medical professionals give every newly diagnosed person in the UK. This means that the majority of people who are HIV-positive and aware of it today are on effective treatment and are undetectable – they can't pass their HIV on to anybody else. PrEP provides much-needed protection from those who are HIV-positive but unaware of it: perhaps because they aren't testing themselves enough, or because, for whatever reason, they don't want to know their status. Many people are terrified by the thought of taking a test, while others prefer to live in ignorance. But the message is clear: get tested and get on treatment if you need it because it will ultimately save lives. It's no longer acceptable not to stay on top of your current HIV status. And for those people who are not HIV-positive, getting on PrEP will keep them that way. Why would anybody oppose this? PrEP is the key to ending HIV. And Greg Owen deserves a knighthood for being behind the access to PrEP, and for the 40 per cent drop in new infections seen across London in 2016.

I'll leave the last words to Calvin:

If I could get in a time machine and go back to me in the years before I became HIV-positive, I would have a very long conversation with myself. I'm not 100 per cent sure the advice would be enough to stop the younger me heading down the path of drug use and chemsex, but I would at least have it in my head that my future health would be dramatically changed if I don't spend more time thinking about my sexual health.

I wish I'd had access to PrEP. I wouldn't be HIV-positive today if I had.

9

BOY FOR SALE

'm on Grindr when a profile catches my eye:

HnH? 19
Goes mad for C

Above this information is the guy's image. He's a good-looking young man: pale-faced with jet-black hair tied back in a top-knot. I reached out to him a few days before Christmas, asking what he was looking for specifically. From the first message I made it clear I wanted to speak to him for research purposes, and assured him I'd keep his image/location specifics confidential. He agreed to let me into his world for about half an hour via an iPhone screen. In just a few exchanges, my initial suspicions were confirmed: the young chap was offering his body in return for drugs and his preference was for cocaine.

He told me he had only ever tried the whole HnH (high and horny) thing once, but was now ready to do it again and that the first time he'd given it a go it was with just one other person, describing it as an 'amazing experience'. I asked about his job and he told me about a bar where he was working: 'but it's just a short-term thing before I get a job as a holiday rep'. I asked if he had intentions of purchasing any substances should he find somewhere they were available.

'I can't, no money,' came his abrupt response.

'So, how are you going to get them?'

'For coke, I'll do anything anybody wants.'

Coke isn't a typical chemsex drug and partly because of this, and the innocent nature of his responses, I could easily tell that this guy wasn't overly au fait with the inner goings-on of your run-of-the-mill chemsex party or the scene in general. He'd probably tried coke once or twice before – most definitely during the one-on-one sex liaison he'd told me about – and enjoyed the buzz of doing something that society deems 'naughty': staying up all night, having sex and getting high. I can fully understand why he would have enjoyed this and why he might now be looking to do it again. But what worried me about the situation he was putting himself in was that I was aware of how quickly people could slide down a slippery slope and, more worryingly, I knew who he might meet on his way down. He told me he'd not yet used G or tried mephedrone: but right at that very moment, someone agreed to offer him meph in exchange for him to visit.

I felt anxious for the guy, but I didn't feel it my place to offer any words of advice: I mean, who am I to tell him how to live his life? He soon stopped responding to my questions, which hadn't changed in nature, so I assumed he'd taken the other guy up on the offer of some meph in return for his 'visit'. Before he disappeared, though, I asked him if he would accept cash for sex, if someone offered it instead of coke.

'No, I'm not a fucking rent boy!' was his response.

This situation is more common than we perhaps realise: young adults on hook-up apps eager to be involved in an activity that can be easily found on social spaces, often in plain sight, but who are unable to meet the financial costs. When HnH gatherings are so candidly advertised in these spaces, it's perhaps easier to understand why some young men offer their bodies and sexual favours to pay their way. Of course, there is a genuine danger that people who put themselves out there like this face risks, and it's reasonable to be concerned about a younger, more vulnerable member of our community becoming abused. But, in the case of my short-term friend who was kind enough to answer my questions at Christmas, the activities were all due to a personal desire to access the pleasures he had experienced once before while having sex after using cocaine. It didn't seem to me that he was making his choices based on anything other than a *desire* to do something, as opposed to a need. I wondered if he was even just a tiny bit aware of how dangerous the world he was flirting with could be for someone so young.

But let's examine the situation from another position: that of offering oneself because of a need to survive.

In the open meeting 'Spotlight on LGBT+ Homelessness

and Housing Options', held in March 2016 between a number of charities including Shelter and Homeless Link, the issue of chemsex among homeless young people was discussed. According to the minutes of the meeting, representatives from Stonewall Housing, an LGBT-specific social-housing provider, and the Albert Kennedy Trust said:

> The use of crystal meth and 'chem-sex' is growing among young gay and bi men. Young people would rather spend a night in a club or exchanging sex for place [*sic*] to stay rather than sleep on the streets. The use of crystal meth is having a growing impact on mental health.

To learn more, I've come to the London offices of the Albert Kennedy Trust on Old Street to talk with youth worker Nathan East. AKT, as it's more commonly known, is an organisation I have been fond of for as long as I've lived in London. It does the most incredible work supporting and saving the lives of homeless LGBT youngsters up and down the country, taking them off the streets and turning their lives around.

It's named after a sixteen-year-old boy who fell to his death from a Manchester car park in 1989; a boy who had faced a lifetime of rejection and abuse because he was gay. Among its many supporters it counts pop star Lady Gaga, who visited the AKT offices in 2016, while its patrons include actor Sir Ian McKellen, The Feeling's Dan Gillespie Sells and media entrepreneur Lord Waheed Alli. It's hard to imagine an LGBT-facing charity that does more crucial work in supporting those who are most vulnerable. Recently, however, AKT has noticed a new trend among many of the young people it supports.

'I'd say over the Christmas months, about a third of the young men we supported were coming to us and talking about chemsex, and had engaged in some sort of transactional sex where drugs had been involved,' Nathan says.

'A third! That's astonishing,' I tell him.

It's across the board, we work with 16–25-year-olds in general, but I'd say it was mostly the eighteen- and nineteen-year-olds we work with who were talking about it most. Chemsex for our young people is more often than not transactional, but for a lot of them, if you mention it as a sort of sex-working situation, they would be quite shocked. They're meeting people off the apps, and you know, we've had experiences of people being kidnapped, being held in a property against their will for a number of weeks; we've had someone who's been used as a sex slave and trafficked. HIV – we're getting a lot of young people dealing with an HIV-positive status. We had a young person who was having sex with someone for substances; they'd stopped doing it for whatever reason and the perpetrator started stalking them, but he didn't want money, he just wanted sex. We had to get a restraining order put on that person. A sexual assault came out of that, so there was a rape charge brought.

I tell him about the exchange I had over Christmas with the

young chap on Grindr who was mortified by my questions about him taking cash for sex.

'That's something I see often,' Nathan informs me. 'Many young people don't see swapping sex for drugs as transactional.'

Nathan is candid in his responses to my chain of questions. His answers might seem shocking, but it's not his intention to shock or scare anyone; he's simply explaining the reality of what he and the charity are dealing with on a day-to-day basis. I ask him if he has the tools at his disposal to help these youngsters.

Because we are a homeless charity, yes, we can get people off the street and into support, into accommodation and away from the situation. But where things do become difficult is if they are engaging in lots of chemsex, sex working and using an array of substances; the service we can provide ourselves becomes less and less because their risk is so high. So yes, we can support young people, but we are involved with London Friend and Galop for when situations become complex.

'Has this been a gradual issue you've seen unfolding, or did it catch AKT by surprise?' I ask.

There was more of a trend towards the end of last year than what we'd previously seen. It's just the tip of the iceberg. It's literally the surface. Young people that we see who tell us everything is amazing – they are incredible. But then sometimes we see young people who just tell us what we want to hear – they think we don't hear what's actually going on. But there is still a lot more going on than we know.

These young people live in the app world – it's constant. They are always on their phone. We tackle app safety with everyone. I have to, regardless if they tell us they use them or not. You know, these young people are looking for somewhere to stay, and they're also looking for acceptance – their families or communities have rejected them. So it's that relationship of someone looking after them as well. Why wouldn't they want to experience that? Chemsex environments might seem like a safe space for them. Just the act of doing drugs with another person can be sometimes intimate in itself: sharing works [drug paraphernalia], sharing notes: the interaction is intimate. If there's something missing from their lives like intimacy, you can understand why they might be attracted to the situation. But again, many will think they are in control of the situation, but they're not.

AKT says that 25 per cent of homeless people in the UK are LGBT, with the majority living in urban areas like London and Manchester, which are the two locations where AKT was initially established to provide support. It has since stretched further than those two cities, becoming national in its service provision in 2013. But I wonder if it is seeing a curtailing of homeless LGBT youth as equality has accelerated, particularly over the past five years.

No, not at all. More people are feeling comfortable at a younger age – they are coming out earlier. But the generation above them, parents and communities, are not as forward-thinking. When I started working here, I'll admit this, I naïvely wondered how busy it might be. I was shocked. We are constantly busy. And the stories range from someone being physically abused, or being chucked out of their home, to passive aggressiveness and bullying. It's not just young people living on the streets: we work with a lot of young people who are living in hostile environments. I think that's a harder thing to betray ... they're being neglected but they have a roof over their heads. We are busier than ever.

Perhaps Nathan's response is unsurprising. Should we really expect bigoted grown-ups with child-rearing responsibilities to have become any rarer a species, just because a few pieces of paper have been signed and gay marriage is now legal? HIV hasn't dropped off the charts in terms of overall numbers. Gay and bisexual men are still just as likely to drink. And, as this book reveals, we are also likely to want to use drugs for a whole host of reasons that we are starting to become familiar with.

None of these things have become any less common despite the fact that life for gay men has – apparently – grown easier over the past fifty years. Fancying a boy in school instead of yielding to peer pressure; having to tell your mother you're gay, but then most likely having to reassure her you're not suddenly going to catch AIDS and die; something as complex as coming out in the workplace and telling your boss; telling friends in the gym that you're not going to dinner with your wife but with your husband – all these things impose a burden that the general population has zero understanding of. That fact hasn't changed and nor will it. Fifty years, incredibly, has not been long enough to take an entire country, and every area of society, along on our journey at the speed which we community members have enjoyed.

Legislators will tell you that we've never had it so good and perhaps they are right. But this doesn't negate the fact that sixteen-year-olds still find themselves sitting on the edges of their beds, as they finally accept who they are to themselves, before then telling the truth to a world that they hope will welcome them. Millions of scenarios run through a teenager's head before he steps out of the closet and into the unknown to tell his family – the people he should feel most secure with – that he's different, that he's gay. Remember how difficult that was?

So far I have felt compassion for those who find themselves mired in the world of chemsex. But I feel nothing but dread, sorrow – and even guilt – when I hear that young men, teenagers in many cases, have used something that I have been a part of as their only means of survival. Their choices are stark: either sexual abuse or a cold night in the doorway of Primark on Oxford Street. This is heartbreaking. No young person should be homeless. But to realise that many of these young men are homeless because of their sexuality makes it even more heartbreaking. What fucked-up parent or guardian would prefer to see their kids turn to drugs, sex and abuse just to get off the streets, and in from the cold for a few days, and to merely remain alive?

Whether it's a nineteen-year-old with a roof over his head and job – albeit a low-paying one – and who is seeking access to drugs beyond the limit of his finances; or a sixteen-year-old who learns that if he downloads a hook-up app, advertises his profile and places himself in practically any part of London he'll get in from the rain – but only at the price of taking drugs and having sex with strangers – our chemsex culture has facilitated the way vulnerable youngsters are abused, used for sex and become hooked on substances like Tina and G. This major issue should not be left at the doors of charities like AKT, Galop and London Friend. They should not have to solve such a huge problem on their own. Everyone in the chemsex culture needs to help these youngsters and guide them out of the darkness.

10

FUN

Some people will do drugs simply because they want to: there's nothing you can say or do that will stop them.

These people aren't self-medicating, and they're not using their chems to escape from or alleviate the pressures connected with certain aspects of their lives. They do drugs because it's how they prefer to have a good time at the weekend: the drugs are a reward for working hard, doing something well. These people remind us that you don't have to be involved in chemsex to use chems, and this is something that we should continue to bear in mind. There exists also another group which treats drugs in a similarly casual manner. But for this group, instead of seeing them as a reward after a hard week's work, the drugs are simply there to provide a way to have uninhibited sex with people who are in the same state of mind.

In December 2015, Hamish Parsons wrote the following article for *The Independent*, in which he describes his chemsex lifestyle in honest detail, telling those not involved in the culture to mind their own business and let him get on with how he chooses to spend his time.

Thanks, straight people, but I don't need your concern about my chemsex and chill-out lifestyle.

Last year I became single for the first time in my adult life. While all my gay friends were spending their early twenties going out and having fun, I was cosying up to my boyfriend and opting for nights in by the fire. The wildest thing we ever did was puff on a joint at a friend's BBQ one summer – crazy, I know.

But once singlehood beckoned again, I looked at that group of gay friends I'd neglected for seven or eight years and found that they'd all gone. They weren't heading into town any more on a Friday; they'd settled down themselves. So I called in a few dinner dates and decided to get back out on the scene.

At one such dinner, my friend asked if I wanted to join him to a party and I said, 'Sure' – it was Friday, after all. I had no idea that would mark the beginning of a habit.

That was March; I've not spent a single weekend drug-free since. I've never been addicted to anything, but 'chill-outs' – and the signature drugs of choice on said scene – have gotten me good.

The scariest element as I write this, sober on a Friday afternoon, is that I know I'm not ready to give it up; I like it. Does this make me a bad person?

This all started off as what I would term 'classy' chill-outs, wherein nothing sexual was going on. It was just a group of guys getting together after spending some hours in a club and unwinding via mephedrone and G for hours. Some weekends these parties have easily gone on for two straight days.

I found another genre to chill-outs a month or so into my new weekend life: the not-so-classy end of the spectrum, more commonly known as 'chemsex' parties.

I went to my first chemsex party by accident with a friend I'd made a couple of weeks before. I knew it would involve drugs, but what I didn't expect to find upon arriving was ten or so guys walking around in boxer shorts or nothing at all.

We didn't join in with the sex end of business initially. I scored some supplies from the resident drug dealer and made conversation with the new faces that were relaxing on the sofa. I measured myself a shot of G, and became high over the course of thirty or so minutes; a bit of mephedrone up my nose and soon enough I was in my desired state. Am I bad person yet?

The alarm on my iPhone sounded an hour later: it was time to take another shot. This I did, but instead of retaking my seat on the sofa, I wandered into a bedroom and found a couple of guys getting it on. I stopped, a little startled, but was invited to join – so I did. As the chemicals kicked in, it felt amazing. I felt amazing.

I stayed in that apartment for about a day, and had sex on and off throughout with innumerable guys. Then I returned the following Friday and did it all again.

I've not become addicted to chemsex. In fact, I haven't been to a sex-themed party during the weekend for some time now. But it's true that I haven't had sex without being under the influence since I was introduced to this new lifestyle.

But back to being a bad person: am I? Because I really don't feel like I am. All my friends do it, after all, and we can't all be bad – can we?

I have a pretty average job, but some of my newfound friends have important work lives; they're charity workers, doctors, lawyers, and more. That might shock you, but I don't find it shocking or wrong. The only reason moral outrage about chill-outs and chemsex has suddenly been ignited is because this hidden world has hit the mainstream media – and, let's face it, the straight community. It's not because we haven't been doing it all along.

I know I'm sensible enough to access support when I feel I have a problem. At the moment, I don't think I have that problem – I think it's society's perception of me that I struggle with, rather than the lifestyle itself. I'm enjoying the stuff I get up to at the weekend. For now, I'm content.

What isn't going to help is a cohort of uninformed journalists and academics jumping on a bandwagon of manufactured outrage. I am yet to read an article on this that hasn't left me feeling miserable about myself. Mephedrone doesn't leave me feeling this way, nor does G – and chemsex and chill-outs definitely don't – but those articles do.

This is all my choice; I won't blame anybody if it comes crashing down but myself. So why the false concern?

Hamish Parsons is a pseudonym.

The author's having fun, right? He talks about 'uninformed journalists and academics jumping on a bandwagon', a reference to what, at the time, seemed like a disproportionate number of articles in the mainstream press about chemsex culture, which used what felt like judgemental and stigma-filled language. And not a week went by without someone mentioning in the *Evening Standard*, *The Guardian* or, of course, our friend the *Daily Mail*, that this new craze was sweeping London. As I mentioned earlier, every time I read one of those articles they would have an adverse effect. They drove me and others further into our underground world, uniting us as we gathered around coffee tables in our pants, cutting up lines of mephedrone and snorting our nights away.

The article is a fightback: a two-finger salute to those middle-class types looking for a group of people to exploit. It's honest, it's raw and it was actually written by me: I'm Hamish Parsons. When I pitched that article to the editor, I said I had a friend who wanted to talk honestly about his chemsex lifestyle and that of his friends. I had only ever written military-themed pieces for *The Independent*, so to approach them while pretending it was really a friend who was involved in chemsex was not only about remaining anonymous; it was more about my finding it easier to pitch something that the real me had never been vocal about.

This book is actually the first time I have written about my experiences and feelings surrounding chemsex culture while not using a pseudonym. The desire I had to write that article made me come up with name of Hamish: I desperately needed an outlet. Inventing someone – and I even gave him his own email address – was a way for me to get around the issue of not having the credibility to discuss something so controversial.

The article was written with sincere intentions: I wrote it because I was fed up with how our community was being represented in the mainstream press. Journalists pounced on our lifestyle, criticising and scaremongering to provoke outrage among the public with articles that all said the same thing – look what the London gays are doing now – and which made people roll their eyes. We were never offered the opportunity for a rebuttal; there was never a chemsex representative arguing the toss, trying to dampen the flames ignited by under-informed journalists. I wasn't paid a penny for my article, and I hope it served its purpose. I heard through the grapevine that people in the chemsex scene thought it was a good article. When you compare the article with the one I had written eighteen months earlier on gay saunas, you can see how much my life had changed – and this was down to chemsex.

It's worth pointing out that I had been through some pretty terrible experiences before I wrote my piece for *The Independent,* and this meant that I failed to take a step back and properly assess some of the choices I was making. For example, I wrote it after the August bank holiday weekend when I woke up to find a stranger having sex with me. But my time in the chemsex world was to draw to a close very soon after the Hamish Parsons piece was published and we'll look at why that was a bit later. But the article is defiant. It's strong and it's confidently saying, 'I'm fine. Mind your own business and leave me to it,' which was basically how I felt at that point in my life.

A friend from the chemsex scene discussed 'choices' with me over a coffee one Saturday morning in March 2017. We laughed a little at the thought of us both being sober, well-rested and in the 'real world' so early on a weekend morning. This led us to discuss how many weekends we had, as I put it, 'wasted away' while dancing around somebody's living room to Jess Glynne while high on drugs. My friend still fondly remembered those fun-filled weekends.

'I have zero regrets about all that partying. We had a great time. Those who allow it to spill over and affect their normal lives, they're the ones who should take stock of what they are doing.'

I pointed out that most people in chemsex culture, and even those who just regularly enjoy chill-outs – non-sexual gatherings fuelled by the same drugs – are single, and that perhaps he, settled in a relationship, could view the activities differently because his 'life' away from them was more fruitful than most. 'Yes, maybe,' he agreed, 'but I still have to go to work, I still have to get up at 8 a.m. on a Monday and get on the Tube. Just because I have a boyfriend doesn't mean that I am better equipped to compartmentalise my partying more than those without a relationship.'

Matthew Hodson from Aidsmap has spoken about gay men

and their attitudes to sex and drugs, describing the 'hetero-sexism' we encounter when children as part of the reason why many of us become more interested in exploring the physical side of relationships than our straight cousins. For *FS Magazine*, he wrote:

> Often we are told that the reason that gay men take drugs, abuse alcohol or have lots of random hook-ups is because we don't really like ourselves; that the casual homophobia we have been subjected to in our childhood has been internalised, and so we seek to escape by losing ourselves in sex and drugs and rock 'n' roll. I think that's part of the story but I'm not convinced it's the whole one. Alongside the heterosexism, or worse, that we encounter as children, we also hear traditional fairy stories with princes seeking adventures, battling dragons and slashing their way through enchanted forests, while the princesses sleep or keep house for dwarves until they are rescued. We grow up subjected to soaps and sitcoms which tell us that women are looking for a life partner but men are just looking for sex, keen to keep sowing their seed as widely, and for as long, as possible. So in our gay world, where we have all been raised with the idea that, as men, our goal is to have as much sex with as many people as we possibly can, is it any wonder that so many of us do?

Another key reason for our appetite for partying, which is also touched upon by Matthew, is the lack of ultimate responsibility

– that of caring for a child – which many of us don't have to worry about. But his article then makes an interesting point on gay men and their motivation for using drugs – that of simply wanting to have fun.

Similarly, some gay men use drugs to escape, because they feel unable to cope with their lives. But we should not lose sight of the main reason that many gay men take drugs – because, just like our heterosexual brothers and sisters filling the clubs in Ibiza or Ayia Napa, we think they're fun. We're on a hiding to nothing if we try to consider the health needs of gay men as if we are all part of one homogenous community. We're not. We don't all think the same way. We don't all have the same struggles, the same values or the same desires. For some people, hedonism will only be a short phase; for others, it may be a life choice.

But surely, responsibility for gay men cannot just be based on whether or not they have children? Or can it? Do straight men and women stop hitting the town every weekend when they become parents? And is this why we see gay men on the clubbing scene for longer and who are older? Of course, it's not that clear-cut. But generally speaking, Matthew has made a very good point: you can turn off your emails, you can leave your laptop at home – even a dog will be fine for half a day on its own if it has to be – but a child? You cannot simply shut down a child like a MacBook.

There is some credibility in the argument that the main

difference between gay men in their thirties, compared to straight men of the same age, is largely based on the responsibility of raising a child. While one group has to go home and be with their wives and kids, the other, largely, doesn't have either of these concerns. So, fuck it! And as drugs feature so prominently in our everyday lives as gay men in metropolitan areas, is it any surprise that many of us choose hedonism for longer periods of our lives, especially as we have fewer responsibilities at the weekend? It's no surprise at all. And Matthew is right, too, that not all of those who use drugs, host parties or attend gatherings are dealing with issues of self-loathing or mental health problems. Some people do it because they like it; they have no major commitments standing in their way and are able to manage how much they participate. And good for them!

Earlier, we learned that of the 3,000 gay and bisexual men treated at 56 Dean Street in Soho every month who say they are using chems, only about 100 of them take up the clinic's offer of support. Are the other 2,900 coping with their drug use? Are all these people 'fun-factorers', who get their kicks from rewarding themselves at the weekend, entirely happy with how their lives are going? I think not. But a lot of them will be. And that's absolutely OK. It's important that this book acknowledges that some people, like the friend I've just described, are able to keep their chemsex activity under control, enjoying it for what it is when they want to, but are equally able to maintain a healthy distance.

However, these people are lucky to have that ability, and I feel that they are in a minority. I think the vast majority of people who say they do chems and who are involved in the chemsex scene are like I was when I wrote my defiant 'thanks, straight people' article: they are confusing the happiness they feel when high and taking part in chemsex with the instant relief the activities offer from the real fears in their lives. I believe those fears stem from a yearning for acceptance: a desire to achieve meaningful connections with people, and an instinct-based need to be loved; to be 'in love'. It's chemsex culture – not just the drugs but the chemsex culture as a whole – that allows people to feel these emotions. And only when those emotions are experienced do people truly feel happy.

I never once bought drugs and got high with happiness as my main motivating factor: I can be happy while watching a James Bond film or after a chat with my mother on the phone (at least sometimes). But I did, every time that I bought drugs, knew I was doing it because I needed the drugs to connect with other people – who were also high – and to feel comfortable enough to let my guard down and lower my inhibitions. Only then could I experience that wonderful feeling of being a part of something, of being at one with a group of other people – of feeling connected. The happiness you get from all this is nothing more than a side effect: a good side effect at that, but a side effect nonetheless.

It's not that I don't believe my friend, or Matthew Hodson, when they talk about people who are only into sex and drugs because they allow you to have a good time. But I think those who count themselves in that cohort of the community are very slim in number – they're the fortunate ones! The me at the time of penning that article for *The Independent* was in the mode of 'fuck it, I'm having a great time'. I truly believed that my choice of weekend hobby was solely motivated by me preferring to do one thing rather than another. Only that wasn't the real situation.

By the time I eventually pulled myself up for air, after twelve weekends on the bounce at parties and a four-day New Year's blow-out, it was subtle things like the fact I'd not been for a walk around Tooting Common for as long as I could remember, or read a book for about a year – two things I did often – that made me realise what a dead end my life had become. A month after the Hamish piece came the wake-up call I needed to make me want to get out of chemsex culture and return to the life I'd left behind. And that wake-up call was to come from a place and in a fashion that I least expected.

11

STRIKE IT LUCKY

You know that when Michael Barrymore tells you to 'lay off it a bit' you probably should take his advice.

Lunch with the most famous TV personality of my childhood in the 1990s, and I'm forty-five minutes late. When I arrive at the pub, I'm sweating, exhausted and in a complete mess.

This meeting with Michael Barrymore, once a giant of the small screen, has been in my diary for weeks.

We exchanged a few messages after he made some kind remarks on Twitter about my first book, *Out in the Army*, and I was thrilled when he agreed to meet for Sunday lunch at a pub in Chiswick. There was nothing untoward or romantic about our meeting; it was all planned to be professional: just two men meeting platonically for a chat. I'd felt privileged.

But on Friday, two days before my lunch with Michael, I went to a party. I kept telling myself that I would leave at 8 a.m. the next day, and then spend the rest of Saturday resting so that I'd be on good form to meet Michael on Sunday.

But I didn't leave at 8 a.m. on Saturday; I didn't even leave at

8 a.m. on Sunday. I partied hard all weekend with my friends and then, in my drugged-up state, felt it perfectly reasonable to leave the apartment and head straight to lunch with someone as interesting as Mr Barrymore.

When I arrived, he stood up, stuck out his hand to shake mine and said: 'Bloody hell, James, you need to lay off it a bit, don't you?'

What else could he have said? I looked like I hadn't slept in days, and even though I'd had a quick shower at the apartment where I had partied for the previous thirty-six hours, I must have reeked – I'd got meph and G sweats from dashing across the capital, and they are not the pleasantest of aromas. As we took our seats, Michael politely asked me what I'd been up to. But when I replied that I'd had a late night with some friends in north London, he nodded once and rolled his eyes in a sort of I've-heard-it-all-before kind of way. What an utter shambles. We chit-chatted through the lunch, which was marred by long, awkward silences: I could tell he was irritated by the situation, and rightly so. Once done with our single-course mains, Michael drank up the rest of his pint of lemonade, called for the bill, which we split, and made for the exit.

I never saw him again.

When Michael left, I hadn't even begun to come down from my entire weekend of partying, so I didn't really think too much of it. I thought that our meeting had been a little weak on conversation, and that perhaps TV Michael was different from face-to-face Michael: and of course the trauma he had experienced over the past twenty years might have changed him from the comedian that I'd always imagined him to be. I texted my friend and told him I thought Michael had been a bit off, and that maybe I'd caught him on a bad day. But I hadn't. Here was a guy who, let's face it, has had more than his fair share of hardship; he's someone who went from hero to zero overnight, and who has never really recovered from an awful and sudden fall from grace.

Today, whenever I mention my meeting with Michael Barrymore, it's not unusual for someone to say something like 'Oh, be careful with him, love', which is outrageous. He's never been convicted of anything; he's simply a gay man who was outed by a newspaper. When I was a child, sat beside Mum and Dad at home in Wales and watching TV, Michael brightened up my life. To have had a chance to meet him, talk with him over lunch and then go away and tell everyone he really is a nice guy – which he is – should have been enough to stop me from partying for just one weekend. But I screwed up. Michael will, still to this day, think of me as a trash bag.

A few days later, during the valley depths of a comedown, I finally realised what I'd done. I had turned up in a mess to an important appointment, without any regard or respect for the person I was meeting. It didn't matter to me who that person was; the key fact was that I had lost all sense of being able to tell right from wrong in a personal and moral capacity.

It was perhaps the first time that I had received a clear warning signal that something was wrong. By then, most of my close friends away from the party world of sex and drugs had each voiced their individual concerns about me and my lack of interest in them. My mother would comment on my Facebook photos, saying I looked emaciated and gaunt, and kept asking why I never answered the phone at weekends. But so far none of this had made me take a long hard look in the mirror and see what everyone else saw. But when Michael Barrymore tells you to lay off it a bit, given the life that he himself has led, you realise that it would perhaps be sensible to take a step back and reassess things. So, I did. I took a few days off work, bought myself a train ticket and went home to Wales.

Getting out of London allowed me to escape chemsex, if just for a little while; the country air, my mother's home cooking and the unrequited love you get from being around your family was soothing. Compared to how I usually spent my days, criss-crossing London from borough to borough in search of meaningless connections, my stay at home felt like a long weekend in a luxury villa. The vibes I got from being around people who genuinely liked me – not just because they were high on the same drugs – made me not want to go back. London was a dark place, everyone was a stranger, and nobody cared about anyone but themselves. Was it time to pack up and move out? Get away from it all; escape; run away? I thought it might be. But then, almost immediately, I realised it was impossible. How could I leave London? My whole life was there.

But life for many people living in London, who find themselves partying all weekend with strangers high on different chems in various living rooms, has to proceed in some fashion: rent must be paid; food, although scarcely touched from Fridays to Sundays, has to be eaten; we all have bills to pay.

Before my descent into the chemsex underworld, I worked for a PR agency on London's South Bank. It was a good job with nice people and a nice office. But as my weekends changed from walking in the park and enjoying a trip to the cinema with a friend, to buying drugs, partying and losing my grip on reality for several days at a time, my professional life began to suffer. Taking Mondays off became more than an occasional habit. I would find it hard to concentrate for a day or two due to the chemical imbalances in my brain. For hours I would just sit and look at my computer screen, not talking to any of my colleagues or phoning any of my clients. And my boss was quick to notice. But, as per usual, instead of acknowledging the problem and doing something about it, I ignored the warning signs. Things got even worse and I found myself unable to concentrate fully on any part of my work: I was merely turning up and going through the motions, essentially stealing my wages.

And then suddenly, out of literally nowhere, something popped up and grabbed my attention. An old mate from the army – Josh – had changed his life considerably since leaving the military and was running an equine centre at a luxury resort in Dubai. We had been in regular communication via email and Facebook and, sensing that all was not well with me, like the good friend that he is, Josh insisted on me visiting him in Dubai.

As with all sudden offers, I initially declined but thanked him nonetheless. But then, after yet another heavy weekend of partying a week or so later, I thought, fuck it: I had a look at my finances and discovered my air miles were sufficient for a round-trip to Dubai. I suddenly appreciated the few dealers who had accepted American Express. With the miles cashed in, my flight booked and Josh offering to put me up in his villa, I ventured over to the Middle East.

Just as had happened when I escaped London to visit my family in Wales, I sensed a weight lifting from my shoulders as I strode through Heathrow departures lounge and then boarded the plane. As our A380 tore down the runway and then soared into the sky, heading off to a sunnier and brighter land, I felt a huge sense of relief. I was unshackling myself from the chains of life in the Big Smoke; freeing myself from the grip of Grindr types who constantly asked for a picture of my penis; from the endless offers of sex and drugs from people I neither knew nor particularly cared about, and who in some cases I didn't even like. Settling back into my seat, with a gin and tonic in my hand, I felt a waterfall of optimism wash over me. I realised there was another life out there, one where I was free from the mephedrone-grip of gay London.

I had a great five-day trip and loved the time I spent with Josh and the people he worked with, several of whom were expats who had left the city for a happier existence in Dubai. I didn't want to leave. As the hours ticked away, I could feel the darkness of south London's chill-outs creeping closer. London felt like a monster lurking under the bed: a monster that was inevitably going to jump out and grab me as soon as the lights went off. I hated the prospect of returning. But, as fate would have it, someone upstairs seemed to be looking out for me.

One afternoon, Josh took me to see a polo match at the resort. We pulled up some seats and sipped champagne as the sun began to set. It was beautiful. After the game ended, a captain of one of the teams wandered over to say hello, and when he took off his riding hat, I was stunned to see that he was someone I'd met at the start of my army career twelve years earlier. We had a good long chat and the following day this kind man, whose name was Sam and who had been an officer in my regiment, took me and Josh on a tour of his private estate. It was all very kind. To cut a long story short, at the end of the week Sam offered me a training position in his investment bank. It was a route out of chemsex: an opportunity to jump ship and start again. All I needed to do was pack up my London life, say some goodbyes and head to Dubai; Sam even offered to pay for my flight. It was incredible. In my hour of need, someone had offered to help me, and I didn't intend to let a chance like that pass me by.

I came home and put the word out to friends and family that I was leaving London and starting afresh in Dubai. But no one was as excited as I was; they all thought I was completely bonkers. My mother thought my wanting to leave the liberal surroundings of London to go and live in a country that jailed people for being gay meant I'd finally lost the plot. And she wasn't the only one to think that way. Friends were genuinely concerned that I would find myself in major trouble, probably within a few hours of arriving. Not one friend or family member felt that going to Dubai was a good idea.

I started to realise that I had perhaps grabbed hold of something that had been offered with the best of intentions, but offered to the wrong person. I wasn't taking the Dubai job because it was what I wanted to do with my life; I was taking it to run away from my problems. I didn't know the first thing about investment banking. I had only spent five days in the alien setting of Dubai, and although the time I'd spent with my friend Josh had been brilliant, I'd seen much in Dubai that I didn't like, such as the way people from India were treated like slaves. I also didn't want to become another gay guy who had to leave London to survive.

A lot of people have to leave London to get their drug use under control. I've seen it often on Facebook; a picture of someone you met at a chill-out suddenly appearing on your timeline, tagging themselves as living in the countryside and 'happy to be away' from the city. And sometimes I believe them. I admire guys for doing it and for many people it's the right thing to do. But I found taking even a short break from the scene in London a great challenge. I felt like running away would be admitting defeat. Accepting the kindness of a person I barely knew, but who trusted me at face value because of our regimental-linked past, would have been unfair on him. It would also have been a betrayal of myself. I was not about to throw in the towel and admit defeat by running away. I phoned Sam, thanked him for his offer, but said no. Dubai was not the answer to my problems.

But going there had shown me what a change of scenery could do. So, over the next two months, I made a few changes to my life. I quit my job. I'd never really re-established myself since my downward spiral, so I thought it best to cut my losses and start working for a magazine. I also quit the place where I was living in Kentish Town. I'd spent eleven months there, and grown close to Murray, the live-in landlord, someone I'm lucky to still have in my life. But moving out was another wise move as Muz would later tell me that his patience had been starting to wear thin: apparently the floor separating our rooms had never been as thick and soundproof as I'd thought it was. I moved down the Northern line and rented my own place, an entire flat to myself, in south London, which with the help of my family I transformed into a cosy home.

Making these simple changes, I blithely assured myself, would put fresh wind in my sails and help me steer my ship in the right direction. But, crucially, the one thing I had failed to change was perhaps the same thing that kept dragging me back to the weekend world I was desperate to escape from – me. Within two weeks of moving into my new place I'd attended my first chill-out south of the river, and within a month I'd hosted a party at my own flat. Despite all of the changes I'd made, with the sincere aim of dragging myself clear of chemsex, I was powerless to stop myself crawling back to the world of drugs and partying.

My former life as a soldier and the different things I did while serving would, as they still do today, occasionally pop up in my new civilian life. Around mid-2015, Glyndwr University in my home town of Wrexham wrote to me asking if I would accept an honorary fellowship in recognition of my LGBT rights work. I was thrilled, and of course said yes. In the early winter, when I was struggling with the very worst of my chemsex weekend habit in London, I headed home to accept the fellowship. The ceremony was planned for Thursday afternoon, followed by a dinner that evening in honour of the other new fellows and me.

After turning up at the campus with my entire family in tow, I was enrobed and given what I thought was the fanciest Robin Hood hat in the world. The auditorium filled up and everyone sat down. I formed part of the procession that entered the room and the ceremony then began with lots of tradition: maces were laid and proclamations read in both English and Welsh. Religious leaders read prayers. It was genuinely lovely, and it was such a privilege to be sitting in front of hundreds of young men and women who were graduating and moving on to their next adventures. I was proud for them and their families. But as the vice-chancellor moved to the honorary fellowship that was to be bestowed on me, I suddenly felt a fraud.

A professor outlined the story of my life – where I'd come from and what I had done – and explained why the university had deemed it fit to award me such an honour. As I stared out into the auditorium, hundreds of faces stared back at me. Perhaps the people those faces belonged to were asking themselves how someone from a tiny village could ever have done so much. I was asking pretty much the same thing myself. But other words were also buzzing through my head: words like 'yes, but there's a side to this person you don't know about' and 'you should see what he gets up to at the weekend'.

As great an honour as it was, and despite the fact that I was bursting with pride at becoming a fellow of Glyndwr, I nevertheless felt an urge to rush off the stage, tear off my cloak and fancy hat and burst into tears. Yes, in 2013 when I had left the army I had been someone. But right at that moment, sitting in front of all those students, I felt like a bad guy waiting to be unmasked: someone pretending to be something and someone that he wasn't. I felt desperately unhappy. I stuck it out, though: what else could I do? I gave my speech, which was interrupted by me needing to blow my nose frequently, and then had a lovely dinner to which I took my mother.

But the following morning, just like an incurable drunk reaches for the next bottle, I returned to London and the darkness of my world: I headed straight to a chemsex party. My forty-eight hours in Wales had placed so much pressure on my shoulders that I needed some way to release it.

Now, it might seem that what was lacking on each occasion I've referenced here was the motivation to do something positive and alter my behaviour. But despite the shame I felt when I turned up trashed for lunch with Michael Barrymore; or my relief at getting out of London and seeing friends, which had shown me that life did not have to be limited to the capital; or the shame I'd felt at being held up as some sort of a hero by the university – it still wasn't enough to make me change. It seemed as if it was impossible to start all over again. And yet I did. So what was it that finally made me throw my arms in the air and cry that enough was enough?

Before I tell you what happened to me, I want to make this next point.

If you are a person who parties occasionally, or even if you're someone who spends every minute of their weekends – like I once did – in people's living rooms, high on chems and wearing nothing more than your pants at most, that's all OK – as long as you yourself are also OK. If you are OK, then this book supports you. So go for it – enjoy yourself!

But by the end of 2015, I was exhausted. I had aged more in a single year than I had done in all the years that had gone before it – including the time I'd spent at war. I was also sick of all the harshness that accompanied chill-outs and chemsex parties – some aspects of the culture that we've so far not spent much time talking about. Think about how you would feel if someone on Grindr asked if you wanted to go over and join them at an HnH party? You say sure, and they ask for some pics so the other guys can see what you look like. And then comes the reply, 'Oh, some of the guys don't like the look of you.'

That hurts. That kind of rejection makes you panic. You start to look harder. You upgrade your hook-up service to premium, so that you can search further and faster, until eventually you find somewhere to go. But when you arrive at the apartment, everyone stares at you. Someone tells you to get naked immediately and then everybody judges you. A guy offers you drugs and you say 'sure' and then begin to have sex with someone, with anyone, because the pain you felt as a result of your earlier rejection needs to be eased.

Or what about the paranoia that sometimes sets in midway through a party, and somebody starts apologising to everyone in the room because he thinks nobody likes him? You reassure the guy, but that doesn't change how he feels.

For me, though, the main problem was that I was growing tired of all the lies that I kept telling myself: that I would have just *one* more shot of G; that I wouldn't buy any more bags of meph; that if someone offered me a puff of his Tina I would just say no. I was so sick of constantly breaking the simple rules I had made to reassure myself I could walk away from chemsex whenever I wanted to. I needed a kick up the arse.

I guess what I'm saying here is that although the weekend lifestyle of partying, debauchery, sex and drugs was something that I sometimes enjoyed, by the end of the year I'd become unhappy. The lifestyle made me sad. Not any particular aspects of it; not the individual drugs or even the actual action of having sex with someone: the problem was the whole thing – the entire chemsex culture. I'd had enough.

12

PLEASE, *PLEASE,* HELP ME

It's a cold winter's night in February. I'm sitting in the basement of Ku Bar in London's Chinatown with forty or so other people, listening to a man recite a poem. The poem, like the dimly lit room, is dark: dark in nature, dark in content. 'Dark' sums up the facial expressions of the people standing all around me, too: some look agog, others are hanging on the poet's every word; some people are nodding, others recording the performance on their phones.

The poem is about a guy roaming the suburbs of south London, going from address to address, looking for new drugs and new people to connect with while high, and for new sexual partners to share intimacy with.

The guy in the poem is fixated on finding more strangers, finding more drugs. The poet ends his recital by telling his attentive audience that the poem is autobiographical: he's telling a room full of strangers he is addicted to chemsex parties and is losing control over many areas of his young life. When he finishes talking, everyone in the room bursts into rapturous applause. In many people's eyes, mine included, there are tears.

I'm at a night called 'Let's Talk About Gay Sex & Drugs', a monthly open-mic event which gives people a platform to get up and talk, sing, act or recite poetry about sex, relationships, gay life in general and, as the name suggests, drugs. It's organised by Patrick Cash, who has become somewhat of an icon in the community for giving people this chance to stand up and get whatever it is they want to get off their chests. And it works. People stand up and talk, freely and without fear of judgement, about subjects that might be considered taboo elsewhere.

Patrick introduces the next performance: two actors who are going to perform a scene from Patrick's own forthcoming play, *The Chemsex Monologues*. Just as happened with the poet, when the actors finish their scene, everyone claps. It's a remarkable thing. In this room a community exists; people are nice to each other. It's like a chemsex party, only without the chems and the sex. People find intimacy and companionship at this literary event in a bar in Soho. It's fascinating.

Sat in the front row is David Stuart, someone who has played a central role in bringing the chemsex culture out into the open and, as we have already learned, someone who dedicates his life to helping people with chem addictions. He congratulates everyone as they leave the stage, and it becomes obvious to me that many people in the room are people he knows well; they are people he works with in his day-to-day role of helping those who want support in this aspect of their lives. I'm moved to see that David's interest in his work extends beyond office hours. This guy truly cares.

The event is supported by 56 Dean Street, and counts *Boyz* magazine and *Attitude* as media partners. Each month there are a number of guest speakers, with the remainder of the three-hour event divided up into five-minute spots when people get up and do their thing. Nothing is off limits; the only rules are based on respect for those in front of the mic. In between each performance, Patrick stands up and tells the audience about organisations like 56 Dean Street, Antidote and GMFA: places where people can go for support or simply to learn more about chems.

The entire event, from start to end, attempts to destigmatise drug use in a sexual setting. By providing people with space and respect to talk about anything they want, people's own drug behaviour is normalised. Some people might prefer to attend an AA-type meeting. But sitting in a circle and telling strangers about a personal addiction is daunting for others. What this trendy literary night in the heart of London's gay community does is provide peer-led support and reassurance that, arguably, is far more effective than any lectures from doctors, drug counsellors, friends or traditional support groups. As people talk, or in some cases sing, about things which are deep and dark, I feel reassured that such events have not just happened to me.

Three hours later and having heard it all – from a chap talking about his cruising habits on Hampstead Heath, to someone revealing that they live in fear of falling in love – it's time to head back to south London. I feel energised and take home some of the love that was so overtly shared in the safety of the 'Let's Talk About Gay Sex & Drugs' event.

'When making a short documentary about the "Let's Talk" event recently, we asked people what they liked about the night and, alongside community support and empathy, the same phrase kept coming up: you're not alone,' Patrick tells me some weeks later, over a cup of tea.

The way we have treated drugs in this country and the Western world has entailed a silencing of truth about these issues. Drugs and drug users are relayed to us by the media as morally repugnant, if oddly glamorous, super-villains. So, if you're struggling with chem use, it's easy to feel like you're alone. Of course, you're not alone. 'Let's Talk About Gay Sex & Drugs' enables an honest conversation about chem use and, perhaps more crucially, about the underlying reasons for chem use. Via simply speaking and listening to one another, we can facilitate greater understanding within the gay community. We begin to combat isolation, low self-worth and internalised homophobia. All these things are common factors for harmful drug use. And I think the key word here is 'harmful'. We're not here to demonise drugs, nor wag patronising fingers at drug users. Drug use has been a part of human culture since the Bacchae danced in the hedonistic hills of ancient Athens. People are never going to stop using drugs for pleasure. But if people are using drugs for the wrong reasons, and causing themselves harm, we're here to listen.

During my visit to 'Let's Talk', I bumped into a person I'd dated for a handful of weeks in 2016. It hadn't worked out for various reasons, but during our courtship we had discussed our mutual drug use, and shared stories of how dark life had sometimes become when we were involved in chemsex. We had both escaped from the world of chemsex, but we accepted that we still too often fell off the wagon as far as general drug use was concerned. Although we'd both pulled ourselves out of the dark underbelly of London's drug culture, we were still using socially.

Now, six months later, my former friend tells me that he has gone down the road of abstinence and stopped using chems altogether and that David Stuart is supporting him on this journey to a life away from drugs. I congratulate him and wish him well, but he leaves me wondering about the different routes people decide to take to get their drug use, or abuse as it often becomes, under control. Is it easier to simply cut drugs out of your life once and for all? Is it possible to kick your addiction and to only use drugs occasionally and within a controlled environment?

'Abstinence doesn't always have to be the answer. Unless you want it to be,' David Stuart tells me.

To be frank, it's a very rare thing that someone comes to me seeking abstinence as a committed goal. Sometimes that might be the case on Monday, but by Thursday when the comedown is over, that commitment to abstinence is gone. It's difficult for gay men in particular, I believe; recreational drugs are a part of our history, how we communed during the AIDS crisis, how we played and shagged during our fight for equality. Chems are a part of how we spend our weekends, a normal part of our online hooking-up negotiations, and the prospect of abstinence could, for some, represent a change of lifestyle and culture that threatens to leave them alone, single and sexless, a pariah among their regular network and rejected on Grindr. Abstinence can be a frightening prospect for some gay men; we don't hear an honest, committed request for support with abstinence very often. But we do get thousands wanting to take longer breaks between use, or to play more safely. To learn how to have (and enjoy) sober sex, how to make the role sex plays in their life more of a satisfying one, holistically. Taking a break from chems (sometimes Grindr and sex as well), while exploring their sex lives with support from a professional or peer, seems to be the most popular request for help we get. And the one that delivers more successful outcomes.

David points me in the direction of his website, where there are online chemsex care plans for anybody to follow. On the matter of abstinence, he's right: of course he is. I know I have the sort of personality that purposely does the opposite to what I'm told to do sometimes, particularly when someone tells me I can't do something, or tries to get me to stop doing something altogether. Call me troublesome, but if you say 'don't', my mind asks 'why?'

A person looking to access support for their chem use will typically be looking for one of three things. Some want to learn how to continue doing chems in a safer manner. This might be after a trigger event, like contracting a sexually transmitted infection, prompting them to want to gain knowledge about how to avoid something similar happening again. Alternatively, a person might want to step away from the culture for a while; perhaps they've not seen their family for some time, or they need to refocus on other elements of their lives after chem use becomes so frequent that it starts to impact on their friendships and work lives. Or maybe they are looking to quit drugs altogether, like my friend. Again, there may be any number of reasons why someone would choose to do this: the loss of a job, the loss of friends, ill health or even a HIV-positive diagnosis. But this last option of a person banning drugs totally is the one I find most admirable, not least because it is tremendously difficult, and something that requires a lot of support to achieve. Even then, a person will have the occasional mishap and find themselves using again, as we saw with Calvin in the last chapter. When this happens, it can be tremendously traumatic for the individual concerned.

GMFA, in partnership with London Friend's Antidote service, runs a regular safer-chems course in central London for chem users who identify as gay and bisexual and who might be regularly participating in chemsex. The two-and-a-half-hour workshop is free to attend; all you have to do is log on to GMFA's website and provide some basic details or, as was the case with me, they'll hook you in by placing a well-worded (and well-placed) advert on Facebook.

It was on a Friday afternoon, while swiping through my Facebook feed, that a sponsored piece of content caught my eye: a post from GMFA asking if I was planning on 'Partying this weekend?' and which then went on to inform me, 'Find help and advice about chems here.' So, I clicked. Two Wednesday evenings later, I found myself in a community centre in Elephant and Castle, listening as two men introduced themselves as workers for GMFA and Antidote. Sitting there with me were eight other guys, varying in ages from about twenty-five right up to around the sixty mark. Some were suited in their office attire, others were dressed more casually and one guy looked like he'd just crawled out of the nearest chill-out. But our age, clothes, or the way in which we'd spent that day didn't really matter: the only thing that mattered was that we wanted to access information on how to use drugs more safely.

The workshop began with each of us outlining what we wanted to take home from the session. Some said they wanted advice on how to do drugs less frequently. One chap said he was looking to learn more about the specific drugs he was using on the chemsex scene, and what effects they might have on his health in both the short and long term. When it came to my turn, I said I hadn't yet settled the argument that I was having with myself. Did I use some chems because I simply liked to have a good time at the weekend after a stressful week? Or were they having more of a negative impact on me and should I consider cutting them out?

What was clear was that everyone in the room wanted some knowledge from the experts about the effects of each drug popular in chemsex, as well as advice on what simple measures we could take to look after ourselves better. It was an interesting couple of hours and I certainly felt more knowledgeable about our culture after attending. But listening to the anecdotes from those in the room, picking up on the snippets of information from various people, I got a real sense of how people's experiences within chemsex could be so different.

Perhaps most interesting for me was the situation of the guy sat next to me, a well-dressed south-east Asian in heritage, probably in his mid-thirties, who told me he was there because his lover had started using chems and wanted to introduce them into their relationship. I asked him if he'd already tried any of the substances that had been mentioned and explored, in quite gory detail it must be said, but he shook his head. This guy, instead of shunting away at his partner and refusing to play, instead researched this workshop, came along and took in all that was available for him. Then he went away and made an informed decision. I really admired him. But, and perhaps wrongly, I offered him some personal words of advice, telling him to think long and hard before immersing himself in this culture, a culture that I knew could become very dark very quickly.

Another person at the event was an older chap, who used a walking stick, and who whenever the opportunity came for him to give his personal insights, always seemed to revert to romanticising the various drugs we were discussing. He would start off very authoritative about, say, the effects of G, but just a few seconds later a smile would appear on his face as he reminisced about some of the good times he'd had on the substance. This was all well and good; it's impossible for me not to conjure up some of the absolutely brilliant nights I've had with friends while off our tits, dancing away in a Soho club like nobody cares. But in this environment, the older chap's smile didn't seem OK. And I wasn't the only person to think so. The person running the session stopped the gentleman and then addressed the whole group, asking people to not 'romanticise' any of the drugs being discussed.

A short while later we moved on to the real-terms safety precautions we could take to make drug use safer. At this point, the man at the front of the room introduced us to 'party packs'. A party pack is something, we were informed, that can be ordered online, or picked up in one of the many London GUM clinics – he mentioned Burrell Street. When one of the party packs was opened, I couldn't help but be fascinated by the contents of the small, rectangular cardboard box.

Before us all were a number of different items, all of which were immediately recognisable as drug paraphernalia. There were syringes, with each syringe made of a different coloured plastic in order to limit the chances of needle sharing and so reduce the dangers that go with that territory. There were different coloured plastic straws for snorting mephedrone and powder-based substances like coke or ket, which would limit the spread of hep C, an illness on the rise particularly among the chemsex community, and which is passed on easily by blood exposure, like the microscopic drops that can linger on a straw if the inside of your nose is scratched. Alongside spatulas and other bits and bobs needed to split chems and make up mixtures to inject – things like anti-bacterial wipes – there was also a handful of condoms and a few sachets of lube.

All in all, what you had was an attempt to give people who might be about to get very high on those three common drugs the chance to make their activity less dangerous. I initially winced at the sight of needles, all nicely colour-coded and made to look less intimidating. But as the Antidote drugs worker explained how each piece of kit fitted into the bigger picture of safer chem use, I found myself admiring the clever minds behind the idea of the 'party pack'. Without doubt, if ordered, used properly and respected, these packs would save our health service thousands and thousands of pounds. Genius! To offer a tiny bit of perspective, I have never seen anyone using coloured syringes or coloured straws, hence my surprise at being introduced to them for the first time at the workshop. The only things missing from the pack were the drugs themselves.

The session was drawing to a close and, as a last chance for us all to get as much useful knowledge as possible before heading off to our respective lives, there was an open opportunity to ask any questions about chems and their safer use. This was when, for me personally, the revelation of the evening came.

'Sometimes, when talking about drug use in a real sense, the advice we give might not always be the most palatable, but what I can assure you is that it's always the most practicable,' the man from Antidote told us. 'It's my job to equip you with the facts and the information for you to go away and make safer decisions around chems, whenever or however you use them.'

He had certainly done that. I had always felt my own knowledge was pretty sharp as far as my culture was concerned, but I had learned so much from him and his colleague from the GMFA and this workshop; even from the other attendees.

Then someone asked a question about 'bootybumping'.

A 'bootybump' is when a chem user decides to take drugs rectally in order to get them into the bloodstream more quickly. The most fashionable way to do this is to mix the substance, say mephedrone, with warm water and then, in a somewhat undignified manner, get it into your bottom so that the drugs can be absorbed. At the workshop, a guy a few places away from me asked about the dangers of this, and it was at this point that our leader for the evening gave the frankest of answers. I want to point out before sharing his advice with you that I fully agree with it, and I believe it was more useful to one or two of the guys in the room than all of the other information they received.

The advice was this: if you bootybump and then engage in unprotected sex, the damage caused to the inside of your anus, and the exposed blood in the part of your body that might occur as a result, puts you in more danger of contracting things like HIV than if you had taken the drugs by slamming. Put bluntly, if you're planning on having condom-free sex, it's safer to inject drugs into your arm than bootybump them into your arse.

Now that's advice you won't get from your doctor.

The workshop guys stand by it, and I stand by them for being brave enough to say it.

You can find equally good advice on David Stuart's website, which provides meaningful, step-by-step guidance as well as endless resources. One option visitors to the site can choose is to 'take a short break from chems'.

Let's say I choose this particular option. I'm someone who wants to take a step back. I've had a dozen consecutive weekends of chem use, from Friday to early Monday morning week in and week out. I'm tired every Monday, Tuesday and usually Wednesday. But by Thursday afternoon I'm starting to feel normal again, looking forward to getting home on Friday night, eating something, perhaps having a few beers and then heading to some guy's apartment in east London where I know there will be drugs and men in abundance. I'm stuck in a rut and my social life is harming my working life. Some friends say they don't want to see me any more, and even those who do agree to see me tell me I'm looking pale and gaunt and seem distant. I have acne.

I'm not making any of this up. In 2015, I went twelve weeks without any sleep at the weekends. I stopped hanging out with my real friends and visiting my family in north Wales. I even stopped going to the theatre and to the cinema – my only true loves in life. Everything just seemed to revolve around chem-filled weekends: me switching off from the reality of everyday living and losing a grasp on reality. My life and all the things that made me who I was were rapidly deteriorating. I had started to lose control.

So, let's say I stumble across David's website and click 'Take a Short Break'. I'm asked how long a period would give me a sense of accomplishment – four months, three months; a weekend, a single day? I immediately wonder how many people set themselves a target of just one day as an acceptable personal challenge, but then I quickly think back to when I've been sitting in my flat alone, doing drugs all by myself, and realise that I am not in any position to judge anyone. I click on one month.

Then I get this message:

You've chosen to take a break from chems, and your goal is one month.

Great.

The idea is to learn how easy or difficult this is for you. And for you to experience a sense of accomplishment. You deserve this feeling and it should give you a sense of what you CAN do, and motivate you to perhaps try this again. (Maybe even a bigger goal next time – not too big, though; we're aiming for a small achievable goal that gives you a sense of accomplishment.)

Now we'd like to know what your level of confidence is to achieve this goal, one month without chems. Choose a number from the scale below.

I must pick a number from one to ten: the higher the number, the greater your confidence is that you can achieve your goal. I pick number seven, although even as I choose it I'm busy thinking about that first high after this break, when I plan to reward myself for staying clean for a month. But anyway, seven it is.

Scoring anything seven or above on the confidence scale suggests you've got a good chance of achieving your goal. That's great. It's important you feel you can achieve this.

Now let's get an idea of how important this is to you.

It's important that you're doing this for yourself. (No one else should push you into this – be it a family member, a friend, a partner, a healthcare professional); it has to be important to you or it won't work.

Choose a number from the scale below.

HOW IMPORTANT IS IT TO YOU, TO ACHIEVE THIS GOAL?

Before answering, I think about how often I have stepped away from chemsex culture because of pressure from other people. In fact, it occurs to me that whenever I pulled away, even if only for a week or so, it was because other people wanted me to, not because I wanted to do so myself. And of course once my short-term break had ended, I always returned to the culture, and probably partied even harder to make up for lost time. But on this occasion I'm going to say I'm 100 per cent committed to achieving my goal. I click ten.

On the next screen, I have to identify typical triggers, times during my life when I would have the urge to look for chems and find people to hang out with while high. Everything is covered, but at the top of the list, something that I'm sure is ticked often by people wanting to get a grip on their chem use is 'After work Fridays'. I tick it and I also tick 'Saturday late afternoon with no plans made', and 'Saturday night when alone'. That's all I tick, as, thinking back to when this was something I was doing week in, week out, those three areas were my red-flag moments. I never woke up on a Wednesday morning and craved chems or chemsex; I never started the week thinking I might order something at some point to see me through until the weekend.

David Stuart says that if you can plan your chem use around some areas of your life – like a job – then you've got some level of control and aren't an addict. But I only half-agree. I think I did have an addiction to fucking up my weekend life. Early on Friday night, I would head to some flat in a random part of London and then vanish from the planet until late on Sunday.

David's chemsex care plan asks what my common triggers are: 'When I'm alone?' 'After drinking alone?' 'When out drinking with friends?' 'After clubbing?' I stop reading and reflect that each scenario is a trigger event for me. I resume reading: 'When I feel lonely and miss intimacy? 'When I feel bored?' 'When I feel stressed and anxious?' 'When I feel horny?' 'When I feel depressed?' 'When I feel angry at myself?' 'When I get an unexpected invitation to a party?' It's starting to read like a tailor-made list of possible scenarios that would trigger me to possibly order in a shit-load of chems.

I tick everything.

And then the site asks about something that so far throughout this book we have deliberately avoided – alcohol. 'For some, chemsex is completely unrelated to alcohol; for others, it only happens after they've had a drink or a few,' the site says.

Alcohol has been a part of my life since I was sixteen. In the army, the ethos of going to the bar after work is king. There's no such thing as a soldier who doesn't drink. That feeling of looking forward to a beer after work on a Friday has never left me even now, a good few years out of the military. One afternoon, while chatting with David Stuart over a coffee at Balans in Soho, he asked about my drinking habits, and if they had ever led to me searching for and buying chems.

'We get defensive about the word alcohol. We don't want to be told that drinking leads to chems, and chems lead to chemsex. But ask yourself: have you ever started using chems while sober, without any alcohol in your system?'

In every instance I can muster the memory of, I have found the urge, or been tempted to use chems because of alcohol. I might plan my chem sessions in advance, ordering supplies sometimes on a Thursday ahead of the weekend, but I would never touch them until I'd had a drink and was already partially intoxicated. Alcohol was a major influence in my weekends of madness.

David's chemsex care plan goes on to ask what I could do differently next time I feel a craving or trigger, and setting my mind back to eighteen months earlier, I look down the list and see a great deal of options I wish I'd thought of at the time: 'Write a letter/journal to myself', 'Practice meditation', 'Watch a boxset', 'Get offline', 'Go to a shop and ask the shopkeeper how his day was', 'Be with people who value you'. And then I see the option, 'Think about what you will be doing two days from now – if you use, and if you don't'.

This last option really hits a nerve. I remember vividly that the majority of my comedown periods from chems would always be based on my regret at not doing things that might seem mundane, but which are crucial to everyday life. Things like doing the laundry – there's nothing dignified about not having any clean underwear for work – or checking out a new movie at the Odeon in Streatham, something I do again now, but didn't during my chemsex time; or having a spare fifteen minutes to pick up the phone and call my dad. All these things that make up our daily lives were missing from mine and it was all because I lost days and days of my life to chemsex.

I tick the options I feel are the most relevant ones and then click 'next'.

That's it. You have your own care plan.

If you can, let a good friend know that you're trying to make changes. Doing this alone is never as good as having the support of a best mate. It can be difficult to share this vulnerability with someone, but do not be ashamed. It's a brave, brilliant thing you're doing here, you should feel proud of trying.

Whether you succeed at your goal or not, you now have a toolbox of things you can do to help yourself. Sometimes it's trial and error; we don't always succeed the first time. Don't give up. Keep coming back. Choose an achievable goal, work towards it. Get better at identifying your vulnerable moments, and practise your craving management techniques. You'll get the hang of it. You'll get better each time.

And when you succeed... congratulate yourself. That's important. When you don't succeed... congratulate yourself for trying. Don't beat yourself up. There is an explainable reason why you struggle with this. Gay life, gay sex is complicated, you aren't alone. So, no beating yourself up, just start a new care plan. With a smile, and faith in yourself.

It's impossible for me to place my hand on my heart and hazard a guess at whether, eighteen months ago, I would have succeeded in quitting the scene for a whole month by following this advice. I'm inclined to believe that I would have failed. Perhaps it's harsh to say so, but I know I've been at weddings with my parents and sneaked off to the toilet to bump some meph. I've attended dinner parties and been unaware if the other guests like chems, but cheekily poured myself some G out of sight in the corner of the kitchen. I've turned up to an army reunion with my old mates completely out of my mind, having left a party just a handful of minutes earlier in Clapham. When times were all about getting high and feeling good, an online care plan that didn't clip me around the ear when I fucked up would probably not have sustained my initial desire to stop using chems. I would have needed a hands-on approach.

After concluding the questionnaire on David's site, I'm sign-posted to a walk-in one-to-one chat on Tuesdays from 5 p.m., at 56 Dean Street.

There are other things that happen too, of course, things that point someone in the direction of packing it all in and trying life chem-free, either for a while or with the intention of giving it up full stop. Greg Owen – the champion of the iWantPrEP-now campaign – tells me that for him, abandoning chems and chemsex happened almost by accident.

I found myself caring deeply about something, and working really hard on that something. My life changed drastically in a matter of weeks – suddenly I was the poster boy for PrEP and I knew I only had one shot at it. I didn't want to fuck it up. It was a case of my priorities changing. Getting trashed and losing a night's sleep wasn't appealing all of a sudden, that's the reality of it. I miss those days, but I don't crave them.

I've kept an eye on Greg and his extremely busy life for some time from a distance. His work promoting PrEP takes him far and wide. He appears often on TV and radio, and frequently he will stand up in front of a large audience and argue the case for PrEP. I fully understand how having this sudden responsibility might be enough to scare him from wandering down the road of chem use and partying. I once turned up for a live interview on Sky News a day after I'd pulled an all-nighter partying in someone's living room – I looked like crap and made very little sense. It's something I'm annoyed about and embarrassed by, but it's something I've never done again.

Greg, and anybody knuckling down on a project that they really care about, would be putting it at risk by trying to burn the candle at both ends. But his situation does support an idea that by having meaningful connections in life, whether they are with friends, a lover or a project you care so deeply about, those people or, in this case a 'thing', can be enough to keep you home and dry. Greg confidently talks about how he never set out to follow the path of abstinence, but it just naturally turned out that way because of his commitments. He cared about them more than the chemsex lifestyle he had become used to.

The drug G, which we know is central to chemsex culture, is a major force for many of its users. It's a substance we have looked at in depth throughout this book. We know it's deadly, and we know that the line between having a great time on it and a catastrophic turn of events is very thin. We've read about people losing the ability to give consent and we know about the awful crimes of Stephen Port, crimes that without this drug, G, he would never have been able to carry out. But perhaps something we've not quite yet spelt out is just how popular it is and how many people are hooked on it: and what all this means for healthcare in London.

For sale at around the £1-per-millilitre mark, coming down in price typically the more you order, the substance is imported to the UK by suppliers, due to it being legal to possess if intended for industrial purposes. And people do ship it in, because we party boys can't get enough of the stuff; we go bonkers for it because of the huge high a well-measured dose of the liquid can give – and, as I said earlier, I believe just one shot of this stuff was enough for me to want it again, and again. To do this after just one go, this drug must be powerful.

While at the GMFA safer chems workshop, I was particularly interested to learn that addiction to G can often require medical supervision when trying to withdraw it from the body. In this circumstance, the experts told me, G is by far the most addictive drug in the culture, and people are finding themselves needing healthcare professional-led assistance to get them off it. For this reason alone, the drug stands out from the two other popular drugs in chemsex culture as being the naughty kid in the corner. News of this dependency, which I must say came as a slight surprise, led me to discovering a clinical trial being conducted by Central and North West London NHS Foundation Trust with the aim of assessing what prescribed drugs are most effective when trying to bring an addicted user off G. The trial webpage tells us:

> The trial is investigating how to help people who are dependent on GHB/GBL. In particular, the trial is assessing which medications are most useful when people are trying to stop using GHB/GBL, sometimes called detoxification or 'detox'. The aim of this study is to establish whether prescribing baclofen in addition to

a benzodiazepine reduces symptoms during GHB/GBL withdrawal compared to treatment with a benzodiazepine alone.

You may be able to take part if you are over eighteen years of age, take GHB/GBL daily and want to stop, you are linked with a local drug treatment service and happy to consent to take part in this study.

I wrote to those behind the trial to try to get a better understanding of those who signed up to it, and see what the future might hold if one of the drugs they are trialling works as an adequate substitute for G. It's useful to know how G withdrawal affects your body and how damaging it can be to person's health.

Detoxification is a medical treatment that involves abstaining from alcohol or drugs until the bloodstream is free from any toxic substances. This is the first step in rehabilitating someone who has a dependency on a substance, in this case G. Medical professionals tell us that the most common withdrawal symptoms for addicts are tremors, insomnia, sweating and anxiety. Occasionally, delirium may occur and, in some rare circumstances, withdrawal can even be deadly. It's because of these severe effects that medical supervision is recommended – a physically dependent user can find themselves in hospital for up to fourteen days, being supervised while they go through the process of 'detox'. It all feels a million miles away from swallowing a small capsule of the liquid on a Vauxhall dancefloor at four o' clock on a Sunday morning, which was how this drug was traditionally used before chemsex came along.

I've never been dependent on it. I have taken it on an hourly basis for up to seventy-two hours before, but once the last drop was gone and it was either buy more or go home, I'm relieved to report that I generally went home. The same is true for almost everyone I know on the scene, as well as the using community. But, of course, there are people who are clinically dependent on it and as a result attempts are being made to make cost-effective treatment available to those who need it.

I have gained a real sense of the forward-thinking that is helping to tackle some of the issues around excessive chem use within our community. It's sensible that drug users who feel unable to stop, or perhaps don't want to, can now access workshops like the one I attended in Elephant and Castle and learn some simple skills about using substances more safely. How useful is it that you can log on to a website and be guided step-by-step through a recovery process and be reassured that help is there should you veer off course? It's brilliant. And the way in which a publicly funded organisation like 56 Dean Street in Soho opens its doors and offers a total judgement-free approach to supporting gay and bisexual men – never once pausing to criticise those who reveal the most eyebrow-raising habits – can only be termed a revolution in how best to tackle a problem and give help to people who need it.

But is this revolutionary approach to tackling drug use limited to London and cosmopolitan areas such as Manchester and Brighton? Could I expect the same level of healthcare support in the small Welsh town I still call home? I'm interested to find out.

I imagine that I'm in Wrexham, north Wales, where I was born. I've returned home for a holiday and have brought chems with me so that I can have a heavy weekend with new friends I met via an app. I pretend that it's now Tuesday and I'm trying to find some help, having spent the whole weekend without sleep, high on meph, Tina and G.

Where do I find help?

I turn to the first place we look for anything: Google. And, somewhat unsurprisingly, 'chemsex support Wrexham' turns up zero results. I realise I'll have to rethink this. Next I try 'support with drugs – Wrexham' and this time we are getting somewhere. I am directed to rehabilitation facilities, which, judging by the language used on the website, isn't really what I'm looking for either. What I ideally need is someone to talk to, so that I can get all the things I want to say off my chest, and be reassured that I'm not alone. But a thought crosses my mind: what if living in Wrexham *does* mean that you're alone? Perhaps chemsex hasn't reached the countryside? I decide to change tack and instead type in 'gay men's sexual health Wrexham', then wait to see what the search throws up.

I'm directed to a health service provision that has appointment-led sexual health testing, treatments, contraceptives and HIV-dedicated clinics, but nothing on chems, drugs or chemsex. I've been looking for fifteen or so minutes and, so far, found nothing. If I was really in this situation, would I be motivated to search much further?

But having grown up in the area, and remembering that whenever I needed something slightly more exotic than Wrexham could offer, I would travel the reasonably short distance to Chester, I start again. This time I put Chester as my place of interest.

Alarmingly, I still can't find any information about chemsex support. I'm starting to fear that chemsex is perhaps an inner-city activity for gay men, so there simply hasn't been a need for a care plan in smaller towns and rural areas. If there's no demand then why should the NHS, which is already facing budgetary constraints, put provisions in place? David Stuart tells me:

> I've visited many smaller, rural towns and cities, to support the sexual health clinics with the chemsex presentations they are seeing there. They are obviously not on the scale of what we see in the big cities … often it is more a case of gay men travelling to the nearest larger city, engaging in some chem use … but bringing the associated problems home to their local health service. Smaller, rural support services often don't need a targeted, specific chemsex support service as there may not be enough people needing to access it.

David's description of a typical rural chemsex-associated call for help is identical to mine. But I should point out that I'm not merely making mine up as I go along; I'm recalling the feelings I experienced while in north Wales and visiting my folks, after a number of days of chem use back in London. My mother pointed out immediately that I looked like shit – she's never minced her words in this area – and, as my comedown started to really lay in, as had happened before, I wanted to talk to someone. I was completely alone.

David goes on to say:

What is needed is for the front-line staff in our sexual health clinics (which includes therapists and health advisors, as well as the doctors and nurses) feeling confident to have conversations about chemsex with their patients and clients, and feeling confident to resource online support to best support those patients. In my own work, I've tried very hard to have as robust an online presence as possible, from video tutorials to online interactive behaviour-change care plans and harm-reduction information, so that rural or international healthcare professionals do not feel unsupported or estranged from chemsex support information for their patients and clients.

It appears that you're better placed to have access to resources and compassionate support services if you are in a more densely populated area than if you are out in the sticks. It seems that the quicker chemsex spreads out of these hub locations and into more rural areas, then the sooner on-the-ground support services like sexual health clinics will become better equipped to deal with an issue that effects not only metropolitan areas but also the gay community across the UK.

But things are changing in this area and people who for too long have been isolated from the best advice and support services available may not be for much longer. In March 2017, two leading charities announced a new service designed to tackle topics including chemsex in hard-to-reach areas and communities. Friday/Monday will provide an online-based counselling service on sex, relationships, drugs and alcohol. For the first time, people in rural areas, who have to date had no access to specific support on the subject of substance misuse and sex, will now have a place to turn to for help.

Reporting on Friday/Monday's launch, *Boyz* magazine said: 'It is hoped the digital services, including an online support group and one-to-one virtual counselling, will make it easier for men in rural areas to take the first steps into regaining control, in a safe and non-judgmental space.' The uptake and impact of Friday/Monday remains to be seen, but compared to the options presently available to people in rural areas – which are so scarce that I couldn't find any when researching this book – it has to be a step in the right direction.

So far in this book we have looked at the routes people typically follow when getting into chem use and chemsex, and have found some common features among different people's journeys into the culture, such as motivating factors or an individual's search to find something missing from their lives.

We've also considered the fun-factor side of drug use and

chemsex. We have established that many gay men are not required to be sitting at home with their partner every night as they're not raising a young family: they can be hedonistic for longer, and some may engage in the culture for no reason other than a desire to have fun. But for many, many others, we know that chemsex can be dark, and can take its toll whether by ill health, like becoming HIV-positive, or by it affecting other parts of our lives, like friendships and careers. We've now also looked at what help is out there and seen how that help is beginning to move beyond the traditional method of walking into a doctor's surgery and telling a person that you have issues. People can these days find help on digital spaces, like the courses available on David Stuart's website, and the new Friday/Monday online counselling service.

But now it's time to look at what motivates people to access this help. When do people decide enough is enough in this culture of endless days of sex and drug use? What drives individuals to stop, and what are the long-lasting effects of the culture once people decide to move away from it? It's time to call a halt to the fun, and find out how difficult it is for people to draw a line under the life that is chemsex.

13

MATTHEW TODD

Christmas 2015 was interesting. I worked at the magazine until mid-afternoon on Christmas Eve, before heading back to my flat to enjoy some wine, festive TV and a probable early night. I like to volunteer on Christmas Day, usually at the LGBT centre in Birmingham, and had planned to drive there from London the following morning, continuing to north Wales once I had put in a few hours serving food at the centre.

But quite out of the blue, a friend in need turned up on my doorstep at about 7 p.m. Tom, let's call him, had been kicked out of his parents' home after pushing his luck a little too far, and had nowhere to go. So, I put him up for the night and listened to him talk about his problems. He'd been partying, had lost his job at the age of twenty and his folks had finally had enough. On Christmas Eve he had nowhere to stay, so he asked if I could help.

Seeing Tom like this, on what should be the one night of the year that he had somewhere to be – I could have been with my folks if I hadn't decided to volunteer at the LGBT centre – really struck a chord. All of Tom's problems were based around chem use, and I felt helpless for him. The following morning, I dropped him near some friends of his in Clapham and then drove in silence for the two-and-a-half hours it took to reach the Midlands, thinking constantly about what I would do if I suddenly found myself without a roof over my head. What if I lost my job and couldn't pay the rent? Where would I go? My volunteering was based around helping lonely LGBT people enjoy some Christmas cheer, but all I could think of right now was how close to a world of isolation I was myself. However, as soon as I reached Birmingham my mood improved and I remained that way for the next few days while with my family in north Wales.

I had planned to stay in Wrexham until around 4 January, and intended to celebrate my twenty-ninth birthday there on New Year's Day surrounded by my family. As the Christmas week progressed, I went for walks, visited country pubs and said hello to one or two old friends. But thanks to that window on the world we all now carry around with us, I could see on sites like Facebook that all my London mates were returning en masse to the capital for what promised to be the mother of all New Year's Eve parties.

But surely, I told myself, I could resist the temptation to go back to London? After all, I was having the nicest of times with my folks. As the days got closer to New Year's Eve, though, and people started to message me, asking me what my plans were, and if I was hosting a party or wanted to go to theirs with everyone else, it started to play on my mind that I might miss out. I even had dealers WhatsApping me, warning me that I needed to get my order in sharpish if I wanted any chems for the celebrations. It all got too much and by the afternoon of New Year's Eve I cracked and told my folks that I'd decided to return to London.

Speeding along the motorway, I could feel the anticipation building: I sensed that I was going to hit the partying hard to soften the blow of yet another year passing. I had phoned ahead and someone had dropped drug supplies through my letter box. I met up with two friends in north London and the three of us travelled to a large warehouse-style apartment in Shoreditch where about fifty people had gathered. It all looked so beautiful: the last year of my twenties was going to be ushered in with a bang, I thought. And a bang it certainly was! I had forgotten the trauma of Tom turning up on my doorstep homeless just a week earlier. I had also forgotten the enjoyment of spending time with my family. I was back in London, and nothing had really changed. I had my mephedrone, I had my G, and throughout the night and into the morning, different guys entered my life, and then disappeared from it just as quickly. My life was back in a rut.

By around 7 p.m. on New Year's Day, the party had moved location and was now being hosted by a friend of mine in north London. It wasn't a sex party in any shape, just trendy guys and gals bopping away as high as kites. But I had already started to put the feelers out on a possible sex party back at my place, or if not as far away as south London, then perhaps a party closer by? Out of nowhere, a text on my phone caught me by surprise. It was from my friend Matthew Todd, who at the time was the editor of *Attitude* magazine.

'Babes, I heard you might be in the area, and wondered if I could just quickly swing your birthday card by?'

I asked the host, and he said it would be fine. If people had been rolling around on the floor naked, I might have thought twice, but as far as I could tell nobody was too fucked, and I surely looked in good shape. I sent Matthew the address and about an hour later he walked into the apartment.

Despite telling myself that I looked in good shape, I was actually wasted. Although not totally out of control, I was high on G. I had just opened yet another bag of meph and, in unison with those around me, had zero plans of calling it a day and going to bed any time soon. Matthew greeted me and gave me a big hug and I introduced him to all the guys. He settled on the couch with a glass of lemonade – Matthew doesn't drink – and we chatted. What he must have been thinking as he stared into my wide, diluted eyes, I can only imagine. We were chalk and cheese at that moment. All around me people were spinning and dancing in their own little worlds, while a few were treading the fine line that using G to the very limits can make you tread. At any moment someone risked going under, and to a person not used to seeing someone out of their mind like that, it would be a disaster.

'How long have you been going, darling?' Matthew asked. 'Have you taken lots of drugs?'

Of course I had and there was no point in lying. Matthew told me how his Christmas had been and outlined his plans for the year ahead – which mostly consisted of finishing his book, *Straight Jacket*, which came out later that year. He stayed for about another hour, but right before he left – and just as I had feared – one of the guys started jerking around on the floor after having taken too much G.

This being a usual occurrence, nobody really reacted, apart from Matthew, the one person in the room who wasn't high and doing the things everybody else was.

'Is he going to be OK? Do you think he might need an ambulance?' Matthew asked.

'Oh, he'll be fine, love,' I replied and carried on moving my friend to the door.

Looking over his shoulder at the guy writhing on the floor, Matthew remarked that it wasn't like me not to worry about a friend.

'But OK, love. If you're all right I'll get going and leave you to enjoy yourself.'

Giving him a big hug, I thanked Matthew for coming over and wishing me happy birthday.

'Oh, I almost forgot, here you go,' he said, and pushed a card into my hand. 'James, how many birthday cards have you had today?'

I looked down at the unopened envelope in my hand and said, 'This is the only one.'

He pulled me close. 'I know it is, James. Now you remember that whenever you go home, tonight or tomorrow, that you only had one birthday card, and that you are surrounded by all these people. They are not your friends, James. Your real friends miss you.'

Matthew's words cut like a knife.

A day earlier, I had dumped my folks, raced back to London, bought a load of drugs and surrounded myself with people who I thought were important. Yes, they were nice people, and two or three of them I did and still do consider as friends. But the clear majority of those I had spent entire weekends with during the previous year were complete strangers. They didn't really care about me, and if I'm being honest, I didn't care about them. Matthew had been a constant friend for several years; he knew me and cared about me. This was the first time I'd seen him in months, and I had been off my head. It should have been a slap in the face that immediately sent me home, thinking long and hard about my life.

But it wasn't. I didn't head home. I took more drugs and made myself as falsely happy as possible. I danced some more, snorted some more and then headed to another apartment with a smaller, breakaway group of people. I allowed the devil in me to have one last party because I knew in my head that something had finally clicked.

Two days later, on 3 January, almost seventy-two hours after I'd started ringing in the New Year, I had finally had enough. I got an Uber home, walked through the door of my flat, messaged my folks to let them know I was still alive, and opened Matthew's card. I still have it on my shelf today.

14

FALL

S o, you believe me when I say I haven't touched drugs since then, right?

Of course you don't. And you would be right not to. But I drew a line under everything that happened to me the previous year, in fact I drew a line under everything that had *ever* happened to me: the army, my marriage and its break-up; my discovery of drugs; chemsex and the craziness that followed; waking up to find a stranger having sex with me; neglecting so many people who cared about me.

When I woke up on 4 January, I looked in the mirror and saw what was wrong: I was unhappy. But it was nothing to do with not having a partner, nothing to do with living in London: the world was my oyster. My working year wasn't due to start for another twenty-four hours, so I used that last day of my Christmas break to make a plan. I decided on four goals:

1. Get a job that I respected and which respected me.

2. Rebuild my bridges by telling my real friends I was sorry and that they meant a lot to me.
3. Tell my folks what had been going on and let them help me.
4. Delete the apps and stop worrying about meeting someone to fall in love with.

I also booked an appointment with my GP, who would, when I eventually saw him, refer me to a drugs counsellor. I'd taken some good first steps to straighten out the problem areas of my life.

Early in January, I spotted a job that I liked the look of, a job with responsibility. I threw myself into getting an interview for it, which I did. I was surprised by how effective I could be, what I could achieve if I set my mind to it, without the distraction of chemsex. By filling my little world with activities, I'd taken away as much as possible the temptation to get involved in chems with pals who I knew used them, or by searching for parties on apps like Grindr and Scruff. I even stopped using a smartphone for a while, to remove the temptation of downloading those apps, or to have close to hand a list of phone numbers where I would be able to source either drugs or sex.

I reverted to the cinema-going, museum-roving, somewhat geeky gay that I'd been before chemsex entered my life. By the end of January, I had gone the whole month since the end of my epic New Year party without using a single illegal drug. And things continued to get better. At the start of February, I got the job I wanted and used it as a further means to continue down my new road of sensible living. It worked. I started my job, got my life back on track, and things for the most part progressed at a pace I was comfortable with. By mid-2016, I could confidently say that my chemsex life was behind me. I was unashamed of it; in fact, quite the opposite: it would always be something I could consider as a life-changing experience. But behind me it certainly was.

• • •

Jake is a friend I met at a party in mid-2015, when things were progressively getting heavier for me. I liked him, we felt we hit it off in the friendship stakes and he's still very much a pal today, along with just a couple of others from the world of chemsex. He tells me what stopped him from participating in regular chemsex activities:

> I reached a low point after a particularly messy long weekend – I think you were there actually, James – and I just realised that I didn't want to be one of the forty- or fifty-year-olds that were at these parties doing the same things week in, week out. So, something needed to change. It was a long process but I found some help, and managed to cut down my use from weekly, to monthly, to quarterly… occasionally lapsing. I did, though, finally feel like I regained some control.

Jake's journey out of his chem use is typical of what we heard from expert David Stuart earlier. All-out cold turkey doesn't work, and as Jake pointed out, there are always bumps in the road. And his journey would see him encounter a few more.

I found myself at another low point: I broke up with a guy I was seeing and relapsed again. That weekend I went from sex party to sex party and ended up at a guy's house where I passed out on G and woke up in a different room undressed. A couple of weeks later I became ill and was diagnosed HIV-positive. Whether it was from that incident or not I can never be sure, but after an initial turbulent few weeks I regained some control and didn't use as much, perhaps just once every three months.

As Jake is my friend, his story is hard for me to listen to, but it's not an unusual one. How many of us keep stories like this close to our hearts? How many of us have scars like Jake, or Greg Owen and my friend Calvin, whose stories we heard earlier? Or like the thousands of people David Stuart sees in his practice every year? Where will all these individual traumas leave us and our community in the future? I ask Jake how he's coping right now, and I'm sad to learn he's suffered a relapse once again.

There's been a lot going on in my life since about last November. I didn't drink, touch any drugs, have sex or even smoke for about three months before, which has compounded the situation for me a little. So, since then I've been going out a lot more, going to chill-outs that quickly turn into sex parties. I've had a fleeting romance with Tina, which made me quit my job and sink into a bad depression. It's easy to get sucked back in and see things spiral out of control.

What does the future look like for Jake?

'I'm feeling good and hopeful,' he tells me. 'I've temporarily moved out of London and will be going away for a few months, so onwards and upwards!'

Jake, at the time of my writing this book, is travelling in India.

Jake's journey, and his lapses since trying to pull away and make changes to his life, shows how hard it is to turn your back on a culture as popular as chemsex. He talks honestly about his struggles, and we notice familiar characteristics in his brave story: a break-up leading him to want to access chemsex, going under and someone having sex with him without consent, depression and HIV. Jake's story is a very personal one and I'm grateful that he shared it with me. But his story is also a very common one. There are thousands of us who are trying to pick up the pieces of lives that chemsex has broken, and we are all of us destined to slip up every now and again as we negotiate our way forward into a brighter future.

Following my decision to call a halt to chemsex and stop using chems, I have had a few minor relapses. Sometimes, it's just been for twelve hours, and I've quickly gotten hold of myself and rescued the situation. Sometimes it's been longer and I've found myself needing to speak with a counsellor, or somebody else I trusted. But only once have I had what I would call a 'major' relapse, a prolonged period that at its worst led me to places in my mind where I had never been. Indeed, the relapse I'm about to recall was worse than any single party, long weekend or even multi-day drug-using period I'd had throughout all my time in the world of drugs and sex. And it came towards the end of writing this book, in March 2017.

It started as a normal Friday. I'd agreed to meet a friend who had close links to a group of people I associated with chems. It wasn't an issue for me. I'd seen lots of friends in the year or so since I'd regained control of my weekends. However, this time something was different and all that night I had an urge to ask him if he'd got any chems on him, and if he could spare me any. I didn't ask him this, but I wanted to. And then he simply hit me with it: 'Do you want to come with me to a party?'

Within an hour, I'd bought some stuff. I wasn't in panic mode yet, though; in fact, I felt relaxed. I had resigned myself to the fact I was going to allow myself to do some things as the night progressed, but I still thought that if I managed to get home early enough in the morning, all would not be lost; it's funny how we often break the little promises we make to ourselves.

I got chatting to a nice guy I'd never met before, who took an interest in me. Soon, there was kissing involved, and one thing led another and we got a little more involved with each other: we swapped numbers, added each other on Facebook, kissed and fumbled a bit more; it was all very nice.

But then, quite out of nowhere, a few other guys arrived, and one of them took a liking to my new friend. Within twenty minutes my friend was going through almost the exact same motions with this latest arrival that he had gone through with me a few hours before. Today, of course, I realise my new friend was simply moving from guy to guy; he was high just like everyone else was. But at that very instant, what he was doing cut me; I grew upset that at one moment someone could be interested in me, and then only a moment later find someone better and move on. I put my shirt on, gathered my belongings, said my goodbyes and got the night Tube home.

If we just pause here for a second and examine the situation – don't worry about James, he's safe on the Tube and high as hell – we can see something happening that we've seen happen to a lesser extent elsewhere. In the setting of a small apartment, where ten or so gay men were crammed in and getting high, something that happens every day in London's gay community happened to me, but with ten times the magnification. I was chatting away, dancing, being intimate and sharing minor sexual contact with a nice guy. My excitement was intensified because chemsex drugs, on this occasion G and meph, heightened my feelings of connection and love. For about an hour I felt like this guy could be more than just a fuck, ridiculous as that might sound. But that's the euphoric feeling those substances give you: it's why we take them, after all. In an environment where everything is altered by the effects of drugs, for me to be dropped and then made to watch as the guy took a sudden interest in a new arrival was a traumatic experience. It isn't traumatic now, as I sit at my desk typing away blissfully on a Sunday morning, but at that precise moment, with all the pressure of needing to be accepted by a small group and feel that I belonged, it was crushing. When I got off the Tube I looked in my pocket and found I had an almost full bottle of G and two bags of mephedrone. Because the guy had dropped me in an instant, I thought: 'Fuck it, I'll show him!'

Only he wasn't there for me to show him anything.

It took about an hour of lying on my bed, swiping through endless grids on Grindr, high on G, to get two guys to my apartment. They arrived at about 8 a.m. An hour later, two other guys arrived and I was now hosting a party. In other words, I had completely lapsed. Five guys soon became seven and the short period of winter daylight gave way to darkness. At around 8 p.m., my flatmate finally replied to my messages and told me he would be home within an hour, and we all began panicking and searched for another venue. We headed off to an apartment not too far away in another south London spot, where the seven of us joined forces with the six or so people already there. Hours went by with the habitual topping up of G and the occasional putting someone in a spare room to sleep off the effects of taking too much. More people arrived and occasionally someone called it a day. But not me.

The thing about systematic sex parties is that everything becomes so soulless. For the briefest of moments, such as when a hot new guy turns up, takes off his clothes and starts fucking everybody, it can feel exciting and sexy, but for the most part, we just fuck each other without any feeling or compassion. A few have Viagra-fuelled erections; others won't get them and don't care anyway. But the process of just fucking people because they are in the same room as you, naked and willing, becomes robotic. There is no emotion, and this is perhaps the most depressing afterthought about spending days on end having emotionless sex with dozens of people. There's just no soul. The grimmest picture I can paint in your imagination is this: picture someone getting fucked, really getting fucked by a hot guy. And then imagine the guy, at the same time this is happening to him, busily swiping his iPhone screen as he frantically surfs Grindr in a quest to find the next guy to come around and fuck him. That's how dead the sex is.

By Sunday mid-afternoon I was approaching my third day of partying, was at my fourth apartment and had met almost thirty people. And I wasn't done yet. By the time I called a halt to my activities, I'd visited another two locations, including a hotel, and met at least another six people. I got home at 11 p.m. on the Monday, having not slept a wink all weekend, or done anything but take drugs, have sex with strangers and forget about life.

A day later, I went to see a counsellor. In the immediate sense, it helped, and I attempted to put my five-day blip behind me. I somehow got through the remaining three days at work and battened down the hatches at the weekend to keep myself on the straight and narrow, which, it should be said, worked. I started to think that my life was back on track, but I was wrong. You see, I wasn't really ready yet: I didn't want to stop having my bit of fun.

A fortnight later, a friend was in town from Sydney. When we had met a year previously, we'd hit it off, but of course drugs had been involved. We'd had a lot of fun over the long Easter weekend of 2016 and I didn't sleep at all from Thursday to Monday. But soon after our meeting, and fun, he headed back to Australia and that was that: another ship in the night now steaming onwards to another part of the world. I thought we'd be destined never to meet again. But I was wrong.

The friend, let's call him Tiago, turned up somewhat abruptly in London, and called to ask me out for dinner. I said yes in an instant. That night, over dinner in Chinatown, he told me about his life, and where it had taken him in the year since we'd met, and I told him about mine. As we talked, I could sense the danger gathering all around me, like a lion closing in on a lame creature in the wilderness; it felt so close and tangible. I knew we could have fun together, but I forced myself to push such thoughts to the back of my mind and went home alone. When Tiago called me a fortnight later, though, I wasn't nearly so restrained.

'It's my last week here, I'm heading back to Sydney next week,' he told me.

I invited Tiago to my apartment in south London that evening and no one saw or heard from me for the next five days. What happened? We went crazy on Wednesday night. And then suddenly it was Sunday.

Love was still missing from my life; I'd just become less bothered about it. I'd thrown myself into work, and writing this book. I had barely noticed that a steady, or even remotely regular, guy was missing from in my life. Grindr was back on my phone, and the occasional shag had frequented my bed, but someone to 'sink my teeth into' like Tiago had been missing. I fucked everything off – all my responsibilities, respect for my flatmate and my job – and gorged myself on mephedrone, G, and, for the first real prolonged period ever, Tina.

Tina is crystal meth and it turns up throughout this book, usually referenced immediately after meph and G, as the third of the unholy trinity of substances. But throughout my own eighteen-month drug-using episode, and even during subsequent minor slip-ups when trying to escape from chemsex, Tina had so far never really featured. I knew what it was because it popped up occasionally at various parties I attended, but I'd never really used it. I had tried it a couple of times, just the occasional blow from a pipe, but I never understood what all the fuss was about. Another key reason for my not using Tina to the extent I did the two other chemsex substances was the social stigma associated with it, even among gay drug users.

I mentioned earlier how many people will draw lines in the sand that they'll never cross: some won't try Tina, others will never slam. But everybody happily does G – the biggest killer of the three main chemsex drugs – so I always felt a bit frustrated when people would say, 'Tina is bad, don't go down that avenue.' *And G isn't fucking bad!* The real reason I had never gone for Tina was that, on the occasions when I had tried it, it had done absolutely nothing for me. But, when my major lapse occurred, I gave

Tina another go at the behest of someone who did enjoy it, and it finally got its claws into me.

I had always associated G and mephedrone with the ability to keep you partying as long as you liked, but the longest I'd gone just on those two substances was about three or four days, and I probably G-slept for a few hours in the middle of it all. But when I went on the first of two long benders during my spring relapse, Tina kept me going for what might have been for ever if I hadn't run out of the stuff, or if my friends had not intervened.

Just like Jake when he talked about a recent relapse, a 'fleeting romance with Tina' is something I can relate to. Crystal meth seemed to be my only real interest for about a month. I checked myself back into substance misuse support, taking a chunk of time off work to get myself sorted out. I can confidently say that the most damaging drug on the chemsex scene is Tina; once crystal meth has you in its grip, it becomes hard for you to decide when enough is enough. And Tina will creep up on you and grab you when you're least expecting it. This is something I never knew until it happened to me.

But I was lucky to have friends who had been there, some of whom – like Greg Owen – were able to reassure me that it's all part of the journey and who told me not to beat myself up about it. Just like Jake, I'm now feeling positive and hopeful, and perhaps I should be realistic and admit that one major relapse in a year isn't the end of the world – and it isn't.

Something that has fascinated me since leaving the world of chemsex is the topic of sober sex following a sustained period of only having sex while high. I was asked the question myself when my GP referred me to a counsellor: 'When was the last time you had sex without being under the influence of drugs?' I answered that it had been about a year and the counsellor then followed up with: 'OK, and now factor in alcohol. How long has it been since you had sex without alcohol in your system?' This time, I couldn't give the man an answer: I didn't know, and I still don't. In fact, ask yourself the same question right now: when did you last have sex without touching a glass of wine or few pints of beer, let alone G, M or T? If you can put your hand on your heart and say 'recently', you're probably looking across the room at your 'perfect' boyfriend. David Stuart encounters this sort of thing every day.

It's about neuro-cognitive habits formed – sexual arousal accompanied by an unnatural dopamine release; not just once, but repeatedly. We are all designed differently, so we all have different abilities to recover from this. Some of us need psycho-sexual therapy, some need CBT. Some just need to get back in the sack but with the right person, the right environment; the right everything. A casual hook-up won't do it, it would require some intimacy and trust, and some practice; it wouldn't be enjoyable the first time. Or the second or tenth, possibly, so some commitment, vulnerability, and a patient and loving partner would be essential. Those are few and far between these days in big-city gay life, so we have a growing number of sexless, sober gay men populating our communities.

David hits the nail on the head. In the app-focused London gay community, it's rare to have sex with the same person twice, let alone ten times. Relationships are few and far between, and perhaps it's partly because of this that the chemsex culture has taken off in such a big way. Since I stopped attending chemsex parties weekend after weekend, I've had to learn again what it means to have sex without the confidence-boosting and inhibition-lowering help of chemsex substances, including Viagra. For those who live in that world of plastic euphoria, Viagra is just as popular as the other drugs. You need it in those circumstances.

Much of my recovery period has been based around studying future sexual relationships and examining how they might pan out: what might I do to make any relationships as healthy as possible? How do I resist the urge to use drugs that might make the relationships seem better, but which in reality would actually make them falser? Much of my recovery has also been based on deleting apps from my life, and some of it on resisting the urge to jump into bed with people the first, or even second, time I meet them. But a lot of it has just been about understanding that my sex life is primarily about me.

In my post-chemsex life I've become remarkably chilled-out, no pun intended, on the subject of sex. But that's only become possible thanks to professional support. The aftermath of any traumatic experience is always problematic. In my life, I have experienced three life-changing events: the Iraq War, the divorce from my ex-husband, and my addiction to chemsex. Chemsex was easily the most traumatic of these experiences.

When we call it a day and decide that this chill-out is the last, or that this sex party will be when we finally hang up our boots, will we all need sexual psychotherapy? Are we all going to have to learn how to get it up again? How to feel sexy without smoking Tina, or downing shots of G on the hour and every hour? How to meet sexual partners and potential lovers without having to download a sex app, or send intimate images of ourselves to a stranger? I'm worried that the answer to all of these questions might be yes. But although I am worried, I'm also relieved that the support is there. It's accessible and grown-up and it can be found in places like 56 Dean Street. All you have to do is ask for it.

15

HE DIED IN MY ARMS

Many of us are on the road to recovery; but sometimes someone isn't so lucky and they don't get that chance. When your luck runs out, what sort of devastating consequences are left behind? Now we are going to find out.

In March 2017, Allan, who is twenty-seven, lost his boyfriend Kris, who was only thirty, to G.

'I took him to his death, James. And I'll live with that for ever. It's hard, it's fucking hard.'

A Friday night in Bexleyheath, south-east London. Allan has been chatting with some guys on Grindr throughout the afternoon, and by the late evening he has arranged with Kris, his boyfriend of three years, to join four guys at a chill-out not far from their home. Kris has been working and, following his shift, he has drunk some whisky.

The pair arrive; among the six guys, drugs are shared, including G, and the sexual fun begins. They head upstairs.

I could tell Kris had had a drink, so I told the other guys not to give him any and to hide the bottle. The rest of us took some, but the G was left on the kitchen table. Kris just helped himself, took what he wanted while we were upstairs. It all happened quickly. I remember playing with the guys, then Kris came into the room, so I started playing with him, but then I went under.

And he went under too. When I woke up, Kris was beside me on my right, and basically, he didn't wake up. We knew something was up, but I'd seen him like this before, so I thought that the worst thing that would happen was that he would have to go to hospital.

Allan tells me this story, battling his emotions as he relates the awful events that took place on that fateful night in January 2017; the night his lover died in his arms.

Someone called an ambulance, and two of us tried to bring him back. Then he stopped breathing. He had been sick, which I had thought was a good sign, but obviously it wasn't. So, for about twenty minutes, we all took it in turns giving him CPR. It didn't help. The 999 people were instructing us what to do down the phone. When the ambulance turned up they gave him shots of adrenalin and some other stuff; they were trying for about forty minutes. They had all these machines on him that were doing the CPR for them, but they said, 'Allan, he's been like this for so long now we're going to have to give up.' I pleaded with them not to. I kept saying, 'You've got to keep trying; you've got to keep trying.' They were amazing, to be fair, they said they'd try for another twenty minutes, but that if he didn't come through they would have 'to call it a day'.

Kris didn't pull through. Allan tells me that shortly after they realised that Kris was beyond recovery, the police arrived, as did another paramedic. 'I was allowed to spend half an hour with him alone, to say goodbye.'

Panicked by witnessing one of their group dying in front of them, and fearing what might follow, two of the guys fled the scene – one of whom had supplied the G which killed Kris.

The police said the man whose house it was had to move out for a few days, just while forensics and that took over. We had to track down the two guys that ran away, and we all had to give statements; it was an ongoing thing. It all just happened so quickly. It was just a normal Friday night, but it turned ugly very, very quickly. You wouldn't believe how quickly somebody could be taken, you know.

I can see the hurt in Allan's eyes. This is an experience he will never forget.

'What was it about that one shot he had?' I ask Allan.

It was because he'd been drinking alcohol. It was the mix of the two. I knew he'd been drinking, but I never knew how much. He'd been at work, so I thought it couldn't have been that much.

I've heard it can be fatal if you're drinking, but you don't realise how dangerous it is. He could have mismeasured – he was
drunk – but no one will ever know. He might have taken some
but not felt it, so decided to take more. I don't know. But the
bottom line is that he did take it and his body just said enough
is enough.

It was his heart that stopped in the end; they couldn't get it
beating again. He was just lying there naked on the floor.

I'm struck by Allan's description of how Kris's life came to
an end. It's heartbreaking. We all wonder, at some time or
another, how we'll exit this world. We don't know what's
around the corner, and although those of us who have experienced chemsex culture know of the risks involved, perhaps it's not until you witness it at first hand, as Allan did,
that you really become aware of the dangers. None of us
wants to die in a stranger's house, naked, having overdosed
on drugs.

Allan and Kris's decision to attend a party together on a
Friday night is not strange. Relationships are diverse and col-
ourful; no one, absolutely no one, should judge someone else's
choices. All that matters is that that they are happy – both Allan
and Kris were happy.

Kris had had to keep his relationship with Allan secret due
to his upbringing in a devout Catholic family in Albania. This
meant that when Kris's body was repatriated home to his parents, Allan would not be welcome at his eventual funeral.

I rang my mum and my sister; they came around immediately. But he wasn't out. Only his brother knew about us. I still don't know where he is buried; I don't know what was said at his funeral; I don't know those kinds of things you need to know for closure. He lived two lives.

I ask Allan about how he felt giving statements about the events leading to Kris's death, and how the police made him feel during their investigations into what had happened. His response is mixed.

At first they were pretty good, at the time. However, afterwards, I do think that if it was a girl who had died in similar circumstances it would have been dealt with a lot differently. All his belongings that he had with him that night were left at the man's house we were at. No putting them in an evidence bag or giving them to a next of kin. There was nothing like that. I think if it were a girl and some boys, it would have been handled a lot differently. I still can't believe that once the house had been taken over by forensics, they'd still leave his clothes, his keys to his office, his wallet with his ID; they'd all just leave that at some man's house. I find that quite hard to believe.

'Are you saying they didn't treat him with respect?' I ask.

'I think they thought "it's another gay who's taken too much G" if I'm totally honest,' Allan replies.

Allan only knew one of the guys he and Kris were with that

night. He was the only one, along with the man whose house it was, who stayed. I'm keen to find out if Allan harbours any resentment towards the person who supplied the fatal substance, and who then fled the scene.

I don't hold anything against them. Imagine being the one who brought that stuff along thinking it was going to be a laugh, you know. It killed someone. You would get scared, wouldn't you?

I gave the bottle of G to the paramedics, in the blind hope they could reverse the effects. But they couldn't. They said it could be a bad batch, but because six of us had took it, it couldn't have been. It was the fact that Kris had drank half a bottle of Jack Daniel's.

I originally met Allan late in the summer of 2016, some six months before the tragic events of the night of 3 March. He is a popular chap, and we share a few mutual friends. I asked him if he'd noticed a difference among our G-using friends since hearing about Kris's death and the events that Allan himself had been through in trying to bring Kris round.

I've seen the guy I knew from the party that night, the one who stayed with me, and he doesn't take it any more. It's scared the life out of him. He won't touch it any more. And the same for me, I've been around others who are taking it since, and I've just had to leave. I'm scared about what could happen. You think they look fine, but they might not be. The trouble is, James, once it's in you, it's in you. With other drugs, they can give you things to bring you out of it.

Those of us involved in the chemsex and chill-out cultures don't generally advertise our choice of weekend activity to the masses; it's not as if on a Saturday afternoon we post on Facebook announcing that we're looking forward to getting off our heads on illegal drugs later in the evening and having sex with five guys we've never met before. So, I'm interested to hear from Allan about how his mother and sister, who came to his aid that night, responded to being exposed to the very darkest aspects of this world we've created for ourselves.

Not a lot of people know about it. A lot of people had to Google it. It's like a hidden, dark world. People think that gays – it's all rainbows and unicorns – but they don't realise there's a dark, dark side to it. People think that we go to a club, we might have a bit of this, a bit of that, but no one really realises what we do. Well, even the most experienced drug users can come unstuck. It's a case of the body saying: 'I've had enough now.' I mean, if you take too much G, you're putting your body into a coma. Your body is shutting itself down because it can't handle it any more. Putting your body in a GBL coma. I don't think people realise that when they're doing it. I think people just think, 'Oh, I've taken too much' if they go under, a bit like a K-hole. More needs to be done to, well, not understand it, but to know what to do if someone takes too much. Even the paramedics, you could see they had no idea. Then when the third paramedic came, he said he knew about it, and that this was as bad as it gets.

BuzzFeed has reported on the research of toxicologists at Imperial College London. Their findings suggest that in London in 2015, one person was dying from a G overdose every twelve days, in similar tragic circumstances to Kris. Allan tells me that the police who came to the house had dealt with an incident just a week earlier.

'The police officer said there were two guys who'd died the week before. They'd been sharing G in a Coke can between the two of them. And he said, "Allan, a week ago, two men were sharing it in a Coke can, they both died."'

Allan is holding up well. He tells me he has days when he wants to just be alone, and shut the world out, and other days when he's upbeat and feeling OK.

To fall asleep with your partner and wake up, but your partner doesn't, at such a young age for me is scary. That's never going to leave me. That's something for the rest of my life. I can't see myself getting in another relationship if I'm honest.

When I woke up he was still breathing, and right then I thought, 'Fuck's sake, Kris, we've ruined these guys' night.' And me thinking that sounds awful, but I didn't know; I thought, 'Fuck, he's done it again.' We weren't addicted to it [chemsex], but it had got to the point where we were doing it every weekend. It can take over your life.

I empathise with Allan; I know exactly what he means when he tells me the culture can take over your life. I remember times when all I could think about was attending a party. It does, quite involuntarily, become an obsession. But of course, one thing I will never know is what it feels to have your partner die in your arms, the way that Kris did with Allan. And my heart breaks for him, his loss, the culture he found himself sucked into and the pace at which a seemingly harmless situation among grown-ups can change into such a tragedy.

'Do you blame anybody, Allan?' I ask.

I blame myself. I blame him, too, but I blame myself. I wish I protected him more. I don't blame the people who brought the stuff because we're all adults – we all make our own choices. I blame myself because I shouldn't have let him have G, when I knew he'd been drinking, and as his partner I should have protected him more. But I was high. It was my idea to go to the party; I took him to his death.

I miss him so much. He was my best mate, and my partner.

• • •

I've never been at a party where someone has stopped breathing. I've never been at a party where someone has even needed an ambulance, or at least if they did, one was not called. I'm struck by how quickly everything escalated on that fateful night in March when Kris lost his life. How many of us host parties where we don't know a single person in the room? Of the dozen or so I've thrown at my place, where drugs were not just lying around for people to use if they wished but were the only things that people were consuming, most of the people in my flat were complete unknowns – utter strangers. Anybody could have had a heart condition; anybody could have quickly downed some Jack Daniel's before arriving.

The thought has crossed my mind, maybe once before: the prospect of someone in my house dying after having taken drugs. What would happen? But then I've told myself: no, surely that will never happen: everyone is sensible, we all know the rules. Well, perhaps we don't know them. And even when we do know the rules, it's unreasonable to assume that people will follow them when they're already intoxicated, or high: hell, if we are all so good at following the rules, then why do so many of us 'go under' week in, week out? Why am I even writing this book, if following the rules works every time?

It's G that is killing all these men; it's not mephedrone; it's not Tina. It's that little bottle of clear liquid so many of us shove down our pants and carry around with us at the weekend. Me asking gay men out there to think long and hard before buying that bottle of G on a Friday isn't going to achieve anything. But Allan's story of Kris dying naked in his arms one Friday night might. I, for one, will remember Allan's story for the rest of my life whenever anyone offers me some G.

16

FIFTY YEARS OF
EQUALITY. *FOR WHAT?*

We've been on quite a journey. As I said at the start of this book, historic episodes like the AIDS crisis in the 1980s had, and still very much have, an effect on all of us. That crisis is only just behind us. We mourn friends lost, or, if we're lucky enough not to have experienced this pain, we start to contemplate what the loss might feel like.

A crisis like AIDS can create stigma-based behaviour, encouraging us to ask sexual partners if they are 'clean', or to shame people by choosing not to have sex with those who are positive, regardless of their viral load. It's astonishing how many gay men don't understand what it means to be undetectable in 2017.

Have we truly escaped from the AIDS crisis? No, but as everyone will tell you, it's become more manageable, which is why today's generation feels slightly more relaxed. But could we soon find ourselves facing another major threat like AIDS? Yes. If we don't act to tackle the epidemic that is chemsex, we might find ourselves facing the same sort of devastation as that wreaked by AIDS in the 1980s.

Am I suggesting that chemsex and sex parties while high on drugs will result in everybody becoming HIV-positive? No, and if that's how you read this, you've missed my point. But when we think about the impact HIV had on people in the 1980s, and accept that everyone knew someone who was affected, that everyone lived in fear that they or a friend or lover might be next; and if we think about that fear of something terrible working its way through the gay community, choosing victims at random and never slowing down, then you might under-stand the genuine fears people have that chemsex will ruin us if we fail to combat the problem. In this sense, chemsex can be considered just as dangerous as AIDS was when it arrived. A simplistic approach, a narrow-minded view on chemsex, will not suffice: 'Drugs – just say no' isn't going to cut it. That doesn't work. If people who previously never used drugs can fall into this dark world, and not stop for a second to consider the dangers of all the partying, then the methods that charities, healthcare providers, community leaders and the government use to tackle the problem must be different and innovative.

If people can be sucked into London's chemsex world and not seek help or a route out, opting instead to look for the next party and order more drugs ahead of a long weekend of no sleep or food but plenty of Grindr conversations and a long list of new sexual partners, then painting a picture laced with stigma and relying on law enforcement to solve the problem will be a waste of time. In fact, it will be shameful. The fact that people adapt so quickly and easily – and, in many cases, accidentally – to chemsex culture means we must look for a solution based on more understanding; something that is truly dynamic in its approach must be adopted. And society as a whole also needs to become more sympathetic towards gay men who misuse substances.

It is only by adopting these sorts of attitudes that we will be able to make a fresh start, and hopefully solve a problem that is currently heading towards a bleak conclusion. We have already mentioned education, and how it became the bedrock of the fightback against HIV and AIDS. The same holds true in our new battle against chemsex. Society needs to learn that not all of us are happy, that not all of us have our lives set up and figured out in the ways we might initially have planned. That's why many of us long for some of the by-products that chemsex provides – to make our lives seem better, if only for a little while. Education is a key that will unlock what is, so far, proving to be a tricky door to open.

But have we found a satisfying response to the question: why do so many people engage in chemsex? We've explored in broad terms what happens; what motivates people; and what help exists out there if somebody wants or needs it. Let's try to answer this question now.

It all starts with the individual. In my case, I was an individual who had recently become single, was looking to meet new people and build connections, with the aim of hopefully dating and, God forbid, perhaps even falling in love. Why wouldn't this be easy? I lived in a city that was home to one of the largest gay communities in the world. As someone in his late twenties, with a good job and nice flat, reasonably good looking (I think so, anyway) and, (hopefully) a nice guy... surely, I would bag myself a partner in no time, right? Wrong. I discovered that the dating scene was completely different from what it had been when I'd last checked it out. People had become app-focused and didn't communicate the way they had before.

Thanks to app-based technology, you can now swipe the screen of your smartphone for hours on end, looking for a face that melts your heart, without saying a single word to anyone on a long list of potential suitors. Going out and meeting someone has become old fashioned; it's something that requires effort, and that's simply not how the process of making connections works any more.

But does using app-based technology cure a lonely heart, or satisfy that desire to make meaningful connections with our fellow human beings? I would argue that it does not. True, in the space of a few hours you can scout, greet, exchange dialogue, send filtered intimate images, swap phone numbers if you're lucky, and arrange to meet for the sole, or at least initial, purpose of having sex. But generally, once that goal has been achieved, many of us touch the block button and neither you nor your afternoon fuck buddy need ever see each other again. A good short-term kick, yes. But what about the longer term?

And what if you're doing this sort of thing day in and day out – or twice a day? What if your sole hobby becomes talking to people you mostly never meet, or if you ever do, it's only to swap body fluids for fifteen minutes before starting all over again with the Brazilian guy in Stockwell? Where is the soulfulness in meeting these people, sharing something as personal as sex, and then deleting them from your life?

Wiping away the memory of someone you've been intimate with, or at least wiping him from your Grindr profile, is like what Will Smith did in *Men in Black*. It's easy: just one press of a button. And the summary that I have just offered is for when things go well. How many horror stories must there be? How many times has someone told you that you're not what they're looking for? 'Sorry, I'm into hung' – that one's a kick in the teeth.

And we all know how outrageously and shamelessly racist, ageist and body-shaming many people can be when they're hiding behind the relative anonymity and safety of an iPhone screen. Unless you are God's gift to men and someone whose Instagram requires no filter, Grindr, Scruff and all apps like them are a minefield. If you're from the school of hard knocks, then great. If you're not, however, then negotiating these apps can be a horrendous experience. And it can take its toll.

But let's suppose that one day someone does respond to you, and invites you over to their place. They are 'HnH' and at the apartment are a few other guys. The guys like you, it seems, and ping you their location, which is only five minutes away in an Uber. So off you go to a chemsex party. I've seen it happen a million times. Someone accepts an invitation to 'come over', and when they arrive tells you they've never really tried drugs, but within five minutes they're trying a small line of meph, and an hour later they're attempting their first shot of G. I've seen a guy graduate to Tina in just a few hours. And all of this happens because you just push back the boundaries a tiny bit at a time.

Of course, you feel on top of the world: topless gays are on you, people who you've never met before want to access your body, to pull your pants off. Christ! Where do I sign up? It's paradise, yes? If your first adventure into chemsex goes well, and by 'well' I mean that you don't overdose, or wake up to find someone raping you, then of course you are going to go back the following weekend. And that's how easy it is.

• • •

I think that half of the answer to the question we asked earlier – why are so many men attracted to chemsex and spend week after week partying – is that we are all looking for meaningful connections in what have become app-focused lives. Those of us still single, whether by choice or not, are eager to meet new people and form sparks with other gay men; and although you might expect this to be easier in a densely populated area like London, or other gay hubs in the UK, the opposite is true. And that's because the next gay man isn't around the corner any more, he's two swipes away on your smartphone.

So many of us now spend our lives worrying about looking and being perfect these days, it seems only obvious that we will seek the same sort of perfection when we search for sexual partners. And if this perfection can't be found in our immediate vicinity, well, we can always swipe down the page and look further afield, hoping that we'll find what we want in the next part of town. The grass always seems greener. Only, all too often it isn't.

Part of this search for meaningful connections is based on our natural desire to share intimacy with other people. Intimacy can be bedroom based, but it doesn't always have to be. It can be sharing experiences, the telling of a secret, or taking your top off in front of someone; it can be revealing fears, or something as straightforward as telling someone important to you about your favourite song. When we establish those intimate connections, we feel good. And if there's one thing that chemsex drugs do, it's to allow you to feel intimate with those participating in the same activity. And that feeling, once you've achieved it, keeps you firmly planted in the chemsex world; it pushes you to the plate, encourages you to sort out another line for you and those around you. As was mentioned earlier by Nathan from AKT, simply sharing drugs with someone is often an intimate experience. The fact that so many people share a longing and desire to make meaningful connections in their lives, I believe, is key to why chemsex has gone big time for so many gay men across all the age groups; it's based on the intimacy that those in the chemsex world share with each other. Chemsex can be an incredibly intimate experience, perhaps the most intimate part of many gay men's lives.

Anything is possible if your phone has power in it.

But are there any other reasons why chemsex has a hold on so many people? Let's dig deeper into something we have just been talking about: technology. Earlier, we looked at all the things that the progression of technology has allowed us to do now that smartphone-based living has become part and parcel of modern life. Yes, we can all now apply for a credit card, watch a movie and order food by using hand-held devices, but in the context of gay men and how we communicate, there has also been another smartphone revolution. Let's focus on how this revolution facilitates chemsex.

Your companions are steadily making their way over to your flat. Some are 'favourites' you have partied with before and 'liked' for ease on your hook-up app. They are nice, fit guys who don't overstay their welcome; guys you know it will be good to have at the party. You dropped them a message an hour earlier, offering them your flat and a chill-out: 'Want to join us? There's four or five coming over. Bring chems.'

You've got some new guys coming over to the flat, too. Some of these are coming from a nearby sex party, while you've picked some other guys individually and don't really know where they are coming from. I always found that the best time to invite a good mix of would-be chemsex partygoers to my apartment was early on a Saturday morning, because people would be looking for a new place to go. Some of them might be leaving a venue in Vauxhall, while others were probably calling time on a party that had started to fizzle out. These days, thanks to technology, the crucial ingredient for a party – horny men – can always be added quickly. But how else can tech facilitate your Saturday morning chemsex party?

A couple of years ago, when I became involved in chemsex, if I needed a delivery from my dealer I would have to text carefully coded messages. For obvious reasons, it wouldn't be OK to text, 'Hi, can you please bring me two grams of mephedrone?' Today, though, thanks to end-to-end encryption messaging provided by WhatsApp, it's much easier. I can order anything I like from a dealer using this anti-snooping bit of kit. Thanks, Silicon Valley!

My messages to a dealer no longer have to be cleverly coded: 'Two mints and a bottle of mineral water' is no more! Thanks to advances in smartphone technology, an order for supplies can be made quickly, directly and, perhaps most importantly, securely. For ease and haste, I might offer to get the supplier to my property quickly, perhaps by sending a car to collect him: Uber offers a quick and convenient service that is cheaper than any non-public mode of transport which isn't public. Uber is also safe and discreet, and of course it can be easily accessed by your smartphone. I know some dealers who depend on Uber for their entire business operation. I'd go as far as to say that gay men probably use Uber more than any other group in London in the early hours of Saturdays and Sundays.

But let's get back to your party. Soon your guests arrive and start using the drugs they've brought: tops come off, your drawer full of chill-out shorts and jocks is emptied. People are smoking in the kitchen, heating pipes of Tina and offering blow-backs; people are measuring shots of G and handing them around. Jess

Glynne is suddenly playing in the background. The boys have arrived. And then the dealer turns up, characteristically later than he said, but you let it go; he's here now. People move in to get to him even though he's barely through the door and bombard him with questions: 'Hey, can I get some G?' 'How much is half a gram of Tina?' You warn the guys to keep the noise down: 'The neighbours upstairs are in.'

In your small kitchen, the dealer starts to measure and dish out supplies to everyone who needs them. How do people pay? They ping it, of course; just a few taps on a smartphone screen and money is transferred between accounts. It's all effortless, and within ten minutes the boys have their supplies and the party can continue. The dealer leaves your flat and heads off in another Uber, to another party not too far away, where the whole drug-dealing process is repeated.

Meanwhile, back at your place, people are on their phones and searching for more boys who can come over and join the fun. Would any of this be possible without advances in modern technology? There's a good reason why chemsex was never as popular in the past as it is today; it used to require so much more bloody effort. You didn't have a secure line into a drug dealer's pocket. And those dealers were a lot more cautious about who they supplied to and how. You had to meet would-be partygoers in a venue like a club, and then invite them back to your place using the ancient art of conversation. You depended on cabs, which became expensive once you hit the third tariff, or on the dreaded night bus.

And you also needed cash.

It's a hell of a step forward when you can pay for your drugs with your credit card, and when you can simply ping it into someone's account in about a minute. The ease with which all of this complexity can now be handled is a major reason why chemsex has more than just flourished in today's world. It's why the chemsex culture has boomed.

Now let's examine the cost of a weekend-long chemsex party compared to the cost of a 'normal' weekend of big-city living. A night out with a few mates in central London today costs a bomb. Seriously, it's a fucking fortune! Bars are closing all over the place because people are opting to do other things instead of shelling out a king's ransom for a night in a London bar or club. And as well as the costs, you also have to deal with all the drunks. Central London is full of dickheads looking to give someone a hard time for no reason at all. I've lost count of the number of times some pissed-up out-of-towner has had a pop at me and a guy when we've been holding hands while walking along Charing Cross Road.

Ask yourself the question: why would you voluntarily cough up hundreds of pounds for a night in Soho, where you'll en-counter scene-queens overflowing with attitude, power-hungry security staff and bar bills that anyone not based in London would label 'stupid'? Now let's compare all this to the cost of throwing a chemsex party. It might sound like I'm advocating the parties, but I'm just being honest about them – the cost of holding a chemsex party is a key reason why so many of us have gone mad for them.

So, let's examine the costs.

G is paramount to chemsex and you will normally pay £30 for 50 millilitres, but if you are sly, and we all know people who are, then you can get through an entire weekend (and into the week) with that much shoved down your pants. We all prefer to pay £20 for meph, but it's more likely to cost you £25 a gram these days; you'll probably need two bags for the weekend, and if you need more then you can easily buy a third bag later. So if you had intially bought two bags of meph, you will now have spent a total of £80.

You can go halves on half a gram of Tina with someone, or just share the bill with a small group, which will probably cost you about another £30. And there you have it: a grand total of £110. And for that amount of cash you can be happy to your heart's content for days. You won't have to go looking for a shag, either; there'll be ample opportunities all around you – hell, it's why you're there at the party. And everyone's been vetted as much as possible via the medium of a hook-up app.

Something else that is important, and which partly explains why mephedrone became so popular a decade or so ago, is the financial recession of 2008–09. Back then, mephedrone, was legal, and those who experienced it will tell you that when you could buy it legally, it was very good; in fact, some people said it was even better than coke and MDMA. But mephedrone then became illegal quite quickly; it's funny how things become illegal when public schoolboys start getting quick kicks in their home counties' towns and villages. However, making the drug 'bad' by calling it illegal just drove trade underground. Us gays had acquired a taste for it, and we weren't about to throw in the towel; we started setting our dealers on to it.

Immediately following that period of poor national finances, the cost of living in London became a real issue for people in their twenties and thirties, probably even more of an issue than it is today. Speaking as someone who was heavily involved in the night life scene, as a sweet eighteen-year-old back in 2005, I don't think the capital's clubbing scene has ever really recovered from those difficult few years; years when many of us had to reduce our nights out from twice a week to (shock, horror) just once a week. I may be looking back on that era through rose-tinted glasses, but I think a night out in the early noughties was a hell of a lot more fun than it is today. But is it fair to argue that some of us found other ways to get our kicks when we were forced to step back from the scene a little? You bet it is. While the clubbing scene has gotten smaller since the financial recession, the chemsex scene has grown and grown: initially in saunas and now in people's own living rooms.

Droves of us now prefer heading off to someone's apartment and hanging out with a select few guys, getting high and calling it a day when we want to, rather than spending the night in a club and then being forced to leave when the lights go on at four o'clock in the morning.

So what is the final piece of the jigsaw, which, when completed, will reveal why chemsex has boomed in recent years? Well, that last missing piece of the jigsaw might not be the same for you as it is for me: it all depends on the individual. But generally speaking, this book has identified the final piece of the jigsaw as being one of the following:

- A desire to enjoy yourself – aka the fun factor
- A tendency to self-destruct
- A means to escape the realities of life
- Self-loathing

The fact that these vastly different contributing factors have managed to come together at the same time and create the problem of chemsex is truly extraordinary. It's a bit like an orchestra full of musicians; all of them playing different instruments, but all playing along in such precise and fine unison, that together they manage to produce a single piece of beautiful music. But of course, chemsex isn't beautiful; in fact, for those whose lives have been ripped apart and devastated by the culture, it is everything but.

Are wes stuck with chemsex? Yes. I am afraid that it has become so strong and powerful that it can now resist any attempts that are made to eradicate it. We might be able to reduce its influence in the gay community slightly, or to curb some of its worst excesses, but chemsex is not going to vanish from the scene any time soon. Many of the support services out there are presently busy battening down the hatches and tooling themselves up in the grim realisation that chemsex will be sticking around. Chemsex culture is gay culture.

One thing that might change, though, is the way in which

people experience chemsex. New technology in areas like virtual reality, although exciting, also present a new danger to those who seek sexual pleasures while high on mephedrone, crystal meth and G. Video reality is about to become much easier to get your hands on; in five years' time, it could be as popular as smartphone technology is today, and if this proves to be the case, where could all of this lead us?

Will gay men who currently spend so much of their lives searching for perfection on apps like Grindr simply switch to finding it by strapping on a headset and then getting what they want artificially? This book's prediction is that we probably will: because we are only inches away from doing this now. Our interaction with people in face-to-face situations as we try to satisfy our sexual needs is already at a minimum.

Just imagine what an artificial and virtual reality chemsex party might be like in the future. You're sitting on your sofa at home alone, high on G or crystal meth and surrounding yourself with the kind of guys you want. A couple of Muscle Marys? No problem. Want ten twinks around you? That's possible, too; in fact, anything we desire will be possible: who cares if it's real or not? But all of this will come at a price. If we barely talk to each other as it is, think how much more isolated we will become if our deepest fantasies can be realised by simply sticking on a headset and then pressing the 'play' button. It will create yet more mental health problems, as well as depression, isolation and crime issues; issues that perhaps we should start getting ready to cope with right now.

What is the future looking like for those who have already experienced chemsex culture, and the masses of those who are yet to try it but are so close to doing so that it seems inevitable they will do one day soon? Well, let's ask those who are best placed to answer this question.

I've returned to talk to the people whose voices we have heard throughout the pages of this book, some of whom are experts in their health and support fields, and others who have bravely spoken to me about their raw experiences as chemsex addicts. I asked these people the same two questions: where do you see chemsex leading if it carries on the way it is right now, and what will be the gay community-wide consequences if we fail to tackle the problems of the culture?

Greg Owen, co-founder of iwantPRePnow.co.uk:

Drug trends in general change with societal, cultural and 'product' trends over time, as new drugs arrive and use of others phase out. But chemsex is different, I think. This isn't going away. This kind of sex is causing real damage. It's not only a behaviour which gives rise to opportunity for HIV and other STIs, it is radically altering how we engage with each other, how we communicate and how we connect, or don't connect in the case of chemsex. I was once at a sex party, I think it was the third we'd moved on to over that weekend. I was on a bed chatting to a 22-year-old who had just proclaimed, 'Grindr and mephedrone have completely revolutionised the gay scene.' My eyes nearly popped out of my head! I was like, 'Babe, why do you say that?' He replied, 'Because, look, there are eight of us here, all having fun, all having sex and all getting high, without even having to really do anything.' I had to pause for a moment. I replied, 'OK babe, first of all – no, this is not revolutionising. This is reducing.'

When I was twenty-two, we used to go clubbing, we would get high in toilet cubicles, we would have a group of friends we recognised from the previous week's clubbing; there were always familiar faces and then those familiar faces became names, and then became friends. We shared drugs, but we also shared laughs; we shared stories, we shared love, we shared heartache, we even shared boyfriends sometimes, but those additional things were there. They were people.

Let me tell you how chill-outs used to happen, 'proper' chill-outs. You'd go out for a night, you'd get chatting to some people who were funny or hot or just sweet. When the club finished, we'd go to an after-hours club; when that club was closing, the little group of people you had fun and a craic with, or snogged or sucked off in the toilet... whatever... you'd go round saying you were having a chill-out, and you'd swap numbers and give the address and then usually the group would walk to the chill-out together: stopping off to pick up mixers. There were girls too!

Then you'd arrive at someone's house or flat and you'd talk and mess about and be silly. And obviously get high. There was always some kind of dressing up or trashy photo shoot going on. And it was fun, real fun, you met people who you fell in love with either romantically or as friends, but that was the way it was. People connected. If any sex was going to happen, it usually happened in a toilet, but it was usually a case that when that chill-out was winding down, any people who wanted to have sex usually left in a small group or just couples and went off and did their thing. Now, though! Now someone's cock is in your ass before they even know your name. That's not a revolution – that's flipped the whole fucking thing on its head and lost the connect along the way: the connection, the fun, the love and the looking out for each other.

'And the community-wide consequences, Greg?' I ask him.

First I'll start with PrEP. If we can at least get PrEP to the people who need it, we'll at least be able to get some control on new HIV infections. If we can get a good HCV awareness campaign, regular testing and simple, clear risk-reduction information for slammers disseminated among the community, we'll get a grip on that too. Other STIs we'll treat as they become present. That's the sexual health part done. Now the really important part on the consequences of chemsex on a community level is how this behaviour makes us feel as individuals.

A community is a collection of individuals so it's important to focus on people, not the 'community', as it's hard for some people to grasp what 'community' means. But we can all understand how we feel personally and how our friends might feel. We've talked about this, James, we've said what a turn-off it is to get 'Hung?' as a first message or introduction. We also know –

how being sent an ass pic as a hello is jarring. If this is what we are reducing ourselves to and if this is how little we seem to care for the rest of the person, physically and emotionally, that is attached to that cock, ass or face... that's a problem.

As LGBT folk, we are already made to feel 'other', or more specifically 'less': if we then do that to each other, that's creating a double sucker punch. That's worrying, that's a breeding ground for toxicity. If this isn't tackled, it can only lead to poor community-wide sexual, mental and social health. On an individual level, a lot of prolonged chemsex users find their lives punctuated with quite dramatic and serious accidents or events such as a trip to A&E, getting arrested, being raped, losing a job, losing a partner, rehab, contracting HIV or HCV or even death. And I don't want to lose any more of my friends or watch them struggle with any of these issues.

Matthew Todd, author of Straight Jacket:

I'm not some prim morality dictator – I'm not in a position to be – but these drugs scare me because I've seen them ruin countless people's lives. People easily become HIV-positive, hep C-positive; they lose relationships with partners, friends and family; they can lose jobs; sometimes the depression and paranoia can lead to suicidal thoughts. We often get into this the way a straight kid might try a joint without knowing how spectacularly powerful and addictive these drugs are, by which time it can be very hard to get off the rollercoaster. With addiction, you always need more of an intense experience as time goes on, so I would expect things to get more extreme.

Our community is in a mess. All the years of assertion of 'gay pride' don't seem to have set us on a solid base. There is some real darkness out there that isn't written about much: the Stephen Port murders, Stefano Brizzi who killed PC Gordon Semple, rapes, assaults and so on, which we understandably wish to see as one-off, individual freak cases when, in fact, they are indicative of an aspect of gay drug culture which is really dark and dangerous. The drugs aren't going away and I think unless we all face this problem and what's underneath it for many of us – feeling lonely and crap about ourselves – I think it will get worse.

It isn't easy to turn this around but it can be done. It doesn't have to be this way. There is help out there, but we need to ask why this is happening to so many of us. I live in hope that this is a collective rock bottom that might enable us to finally face the damage that's been done to us over the last fifty years and beyond. There are a lot of gay and bi men in recovery already and the numbers are growing. Having therapy and recovery needs to become as much part of our culture as drag, drinking and divas.

Calvin:

I would say that we shouldn't be judgemental about chemsex culture. In no way does it affect everyone, and some people manage their lives without trouble, but we're at a major crisis and for this to be avoided, we need honesty about the issues, safe places to discuss and of course a community that doesn't judge chem usage – especially not ours. If there isn't a recalibration and an openness of discussion then I'm afraid we are heading towards further deaths with the chems, with people on the scene not caring for each other.

If we don't tackle the issues in our community then I'm afraid we're allowing a small group of people to ruin and decide people's lives. When opportunities arise to hurt individuals, especially those vulnerable on the chemsex scene, then some will see this as a green light to perpetuate some of this awful behaviour and leave the scene in a state of mess.

We need to combat that by growing a new open scene within the LGBTQ+ community, which has started with things like 'Let's Talk' and 56 Dean Street but needs more, and this needs to be the route to find a safe space for people to feel safe in the community.

Stephen Morris, National Probation Service:

I think this question invites us to firstly remember that, for some, there will be no change in routine use until they get bored with it or move on to other forms of fulfilment and recreation. This would apply to those who make use of chems safely, are psychologically robust and are resilient in the face of vulnerability.

For those that meet the criteria, then, the motivational factors for use are coming from a place of emotional security, and this will be reflected in the place that enjoying chemsex takes in their lives. Chemsex won't be a dominant feature. They will have other interests in their lives and there will be a healthy sense of self, good self-esteem and an ability to enjoy all forms of intimacy.

For those whose involvement in chemsex is not informed by a positive psychology and who continue to engage without change, then the outcome is concerning indeed. From a psychological perspective, for many people the motivation to engage in chemsex comes from an immense need, consciously or unconsciously, to self-medicate against emotional pain and discomfort. In short, engagement in chemsex is an attempt to defend against all the insecurities, past hurts, effects of unaddressed trauma, shaming, guilt, rejection and identity issues held in an individual's history.

As with all defences, chemsex provides a comfort zone and we learn very early in life to become very attached to anything that creates and maintains a sense of comfort. We are hard-wired to avoid discomfort no matter what the cost. The cost of relying on an external defence is that eventually it takes us back into the very experience or experiences that we were seeking to avoid in the first place. Chemsex does not remove the internal struggles and conflicts; it can only offer a temporary relief. If chemsex culture is not met with understanding, love and compassion then those involved will remain at the mercy of their defences. If this is the outcome then situations will be repeated that invite further hurt, shaming and guilt. If we allow this to happen then we will see more crime, more impaired mental health and more suicides.

'What are the consequences for all of us, the gay community?' I ask.

The fact that this book is being written indicates a window of opportunity for the gay community and its response to chemsex. This book, along with the documentary *chemsex,* the writings of Matthew Todd, the productions of Patrick Cash and the inspirational pioneering work of David Stuart collectively invite us to be aware and to respond radically with compassion instead of repeating the very dynamics of judgement and hatred that have given rise to the whole phenomenon of chemsex.

The presence of chemsex in our community is a powerful reminder that as gay men we are still being hurt and traumatised by wider society. Scratch the surface of our newly found freedoms and rights and much prejudice and hatred remains. If we reject the needs of those involved in chemsex, if we judge and reject them and create a sense of 'other' about them, then our community is guilty of hate and is endorsing attitudes and behaviour that inform the presence of homophobia and hate crime. It's crucial then that we dig as deep as we need within ourselves to engage in compassionate thinking and action. Without such a response we will find ourselves turning our backs and rejecting those that most need a new high, a new experience of love and acceptance. If we fail to do this, our rights have gained us absolutely nothing.

Matthew Cain, editor-in-chief Attitude *magazine:*

I don't think it will carry on in the way it is now. If you look back over history, you tend to find that these socio-cultural phenomena burn themselves out eventually. And I think as acceptance of LGBTQ+ people continues to grow in the UK, self-destructive behaviour among gay men will start to fall. I don't think internalised homophobia and self-loathing is the only cause of the chemsex phenomenon, but I do think it's a significant factor – and as we get better as a community at helping ourselves and each other heal the pain we've experienced in the past and continue to carry with us, then the significance of this factor will diminish.

I feel hopeful about the future and think the first step towards tackling any problem is talking about it. We've already begun to do this, both in the gay media and in the mainstream media, as well as within our community. This book and the discussion it will provoke is the next significant step on this journey. And there are already signs that we're starting to become more self-loving and self-respecting as a community. So, the solution to the problem is already under way!

Before I give you David Stuart's spectacularly crafted response to my two questions, I want to say a couple of things. Firstly, this book recognises David, explicitly, as being a pioneer; a one-man walking, breathing, talking and inspirational hero. He is saving lives every day. He's voicing the realities of thousands of gay and bisexual men, here in London and beyond, who are trapped by chemsex. There is nothing he hasn't seen or heard in his daily efforts to help people and, perhaps most importantly with David, all his work is driven by his own past experiences … it's his own incredible journey with chemsex, with HIV and with living authentically in all senses, that drives his unquestionable commitment to us, the gay community.

I asked David my two questions, and he came back to me saying: 'Not today, James. My answers would be blurred. I'm dealing with a drug death that just happened this weekend. I'm sorry.'

This, whether rightly or wrongly, prompted me to text many of my chemsex friends, in fact any friends I know who are well established in the community, to find out who had been lost. On this occasion, it was not someone I knew. But the brief insight into David's working life, and how it affects him personally, was telling. He really cares. I love him for that. He then came back to me a few days later, offering me his answers, but only on the condition that I wrote them in full, unchanged. Who am I to protest even slightly? This is what he said.

David Stuart, 56 Dean Street:

Even way back when, I knew chemsex was going to be big. Before the film, before the hashtag, before the West End plays, before the health sector acknowledged it as a thing. But I never,

ever, expected or predicted it to get so dark. I never would have believed, for instance, that party-going drug-loving gay men would adopt injecting in such large numbers. Or that it'd get a cute nickname, 'slamming'.

I never thought we'd be seeing two deaths a month from GBL. I never thought we'd have dozens of drug-induced psychotic presentations at A&E each weekend, I never thought I'd be seeing so many gay men admitted under section orders. I never thought I'd hear so frequently the sentence: 'It wasn't rape, though, that stuff just happens at chemsex parties.'

I never thought our bright and shiny sexual health centres and gay charities would be swamped by the volume of poor mental health cases that they are seeing. And I never imagined our criminal justice system would be managing the number of sexual offences from gay men seeking nothing more than the pleasure of sexual pursuits. These gay men are not criminals. They are vulnerable men self-medicating their way through a complicated sexual identity and practice, seemingly unsupported by their communities, defensively and blindly celebrating the gay sexual liberation they fought so long and hard for in this angry new fight against heteronormativity. I never, ever, foresaw a chemsex serial killer, or a chemsex psychotic cannibalistic cop-killer.

Some drug trends come and go. Magic mushrooms pop their heads up from time to time, so does LSD. The 'NPS/Legal High' craze flared up and never really manifested itself as the great heterosexual public health concern some thought it might be. A few decades ago, though, a couple of people might have noticed an increase in heroin use: noticed that it was predominantly associated with poverty, homelessness, poor mental health and crime. One of them might have questioned if this was a passing drug trend.

They'd have soon learned that heroin was here to stay. It served a purpose, tapped into something some particularly vulnerable people needed. They'd have acknowledged, rightly, that heroin was here to stay, and that our streets would be full of homeless, drug-dependent vulnerable people.

Chems, crystal meth, mephedrone, G: in Zeitgeist style, these drugs are tapping into something that many among our gay communities need. Tapping into where we are most vulnerable: our sex. Chemsex is not a passing trend; that much I knew. I knew for certain, and it's the reason I fought so hard and long to understand it; to get the right support services set up and to raise awareness so loudly and boldly, although that very loudness did upset many. I apologise. But chemsex is here to stay, and I fear that our scenes and support services will be populated by highly sexualised, psychotic problematic chem users; gorgeous, vulnerable people one and all, struggling with nothing more than the difficulty of having sober sex and in forming intimacies and relationships, but with the direst of consequences.

That said – and I apologise for being so bleak – I know how resilient we gay men can be, how resilient our gay communities can be. I know this because I've just lived through a harrowing

AIDS epidemic: an epidemic that devastated our communities, nearly wiped out a generation of gay men. It brought out the worst in us, and the best in us; mostly the best.

This year, as London celebrates a 50 per cent reduction in HIV infections for the first time since the beginning of the epidemic, I'm reminded how resilient and brilliant we can be. I see that brilliance in our gay scenes and communities today: theatre, arts, culture, Queer performance; all addressing gay sexuality and chems, generating dialogue and debate and thought, as we, this resilient community, try to figure out what's happening among our most vulnerable. As to the future of chemsex: yes, it's here to stay for a good while. We haven't figured it out yet, but we will, and we'll prevail. We'll prevail proudly. We always do.

If you are involved in chemsex culture, I hope this book has reassured you that you are not alone. When you are ready, there are people standing by to support you: David Stuart's door is always open, as are those of the support services of everyone else we have mentioned in this book. And my door is always open, too.

What's missing? A community-wide open door, a true empathy that allows people to ask for help free from the fear of being judged; an empathy that allows those who want to access advice and who *need* to access advice the space to do so. And perhaps most importantly, we need a community that facilitates the dissemination of education that is necessary if we are to emerge from the darkness of chemsex. It was education that stopped AIDS from killing us all, and it is education that can prevent many people from dying from chemsex addiction. One gay man dying every twelve days in London as a direct result of chemsex means we need to stop stigmatising, to stop turning our heads and denying what is happening right now in our community.

When publication of this book was announced in February 2017, someone hiding behind the anonymity of social media tweeted me to say they hoped I became HIV-positive for the choices I'd made in becoming a chemsex addict. Well, let me firstly say: fuck you, whoever you are! But beyond that, let's call out exactly what this represents: one gay man is telling another that he hopes that the other guy gets HIV – and this is less than thirty years since AIDS almost wiped us out! It's nothing more than homosexual self-loathing and outright internalised homophobia, laced with denial and sugar-coated with stigma.

And that guy is not alone in feeling this way towards those of us affected by chemsex. And this is what must change. Too many gay people spend their time throwing shade at other gay people; I did it once: I made comments I regret about people choosing to have sex in saunas. I'm a dick. But we can all of us change: I changed. And the community must change now.

If you are not involved in chemsex, I hope this book has given you an insight and an understanding into what life is like for thousands and thousands of us who are. We are all around you, but our battles are invisible. If you know someone who is drifting further and further away, reach out and offer love. Elton once said 'love is the cure' to defeating AIDS. He was right. And love is also how we will triumph in our battle against chemsex addiction, and everything that comes with it. Kris was still alive when I started writing this book; his death shouldn't be in vain. His partner who survives him, Allan, wanted me to include the story because he believed that putting the harsh truth about how Kris died out there would serve as a valuable reminder of how important education is for everyone who uses chemsex drugs, or for anyone at risk of picking them up and getting sucked into the culture, just like I was.

Chemsex is the AIDS of our generation. It might not be killing gay men in such high numbers, but it's killing gay men nonetheless. There is so much pressure placed upon the shoulders of young gay men these days: to get a good job; earn enough to pay the rent; get a nice flat; look good; wear the right clothes; date hot guys; say the right things; have sex with lots of men... Is it any wonder that chemsex has spread like wildfire? Of course not. The conditioning of our lives, of that so-called community of ours, and the incredible journey that we have all been on in order to arrive at the place where we now are, fifty years on from decriminalisation – all of this has acted as more than just a catalyst. It has become the natural evolution of us all, and of who we all are; it's what we have turned into. Like AIDS, the popularity of chemsex has spiked, but if the gay community opens its minds and its hearts, it's days will be numbered.

ACKNOWLEDGEMENTS

I'm grateful to Iain Dale for allowing me to remain with Bite-back for this, my second book. In the four years since *Out in the Army* was released I've pitched Iain a few ideas, none of which really grabbed his attention. Then I texted him at the end of summer 2016: 'How about a book on chemsex?' Iain replied immediately, asking me to send him three chapters. He was on board from the start.

Perhaps the person not fully on board from the start was me. I naïvely assumed that writing about sex and drugs every day for six months would be a walk in the park. I was wrong. Chemsex, and my struggle with it, has been the most traumatic experience of my life. And writing about it, well, that's the second most traumatic experience. After that comes marriage and Iraq. But what's a life if, by the time you're done with it, you have nothing exciting to leave behind by way of a tale or two? I must thank Iain and his excellent team, including my editors Bernadette Marron and Olivia Beattie, for making this book possible. Thank you.

Knowing there are people just like you, enduring similar

struggles and fighting the same addictions, is a powerful weapon in the battle to understand and accept personal issues. In London, so many of us have unionised and shared experiences largely thanks to the incredible work of Patrick Cash, tirelessly working away at 'Let's Talk About Gay Sex & Drugs' nights, or one of his great plays, like *The Clinic* or *The Chemsex Monologues*. He has normalised chemsex culture for those of us who felt alien, alone and isolated by our problems. He brought us together and encouraged us to sing, recite poetry, write stories or simply open up our hearts. Thank you, Patrick.

Did you read Matthew Todd's awesome book *Straight Jacket*? Of course you did. Who didn't? It was brilliant and it really helped me, as a gay man, gain a sense of why I'm wired the way I am. But beyond offering me his great book, Matthew did a hell of a lot more, and it's why there's a whole chapter named after him in this book. Matthew, I owe you one, love.

Another Matthew, this one of the Cain variety, from Bolton, is among my closest friends, even if he does occasionally drive me up the wall. He's on point with advice whenever needed, and on more than one occasion he's had to rush to my aid. The ability to make people love you even when you're getting on their nerves is fantastic; and that's what I love about him. You're top of the class to me, Matt.

There's a growing list of flatmates I should probably apologise to, having driven several of them to head for the door once they'd reached the end of their tether with the chill-outs that would occur in our living room every other week. Sorry, guys.

As always, I'm thankful to my English teacher from school, who today is a great friend of the family; thank you, Margaret Graham. Thanks also to my sister-in-law Rhian, for always being just a call away when times have been tough.

My brother and sister, Paul and Liza, I love you both very much; I'm lucky to have such brilliant siblings. You've been incredible through what has been the most difficult period of all our lives, worrying about our mum.

And Mum, you are an inspiration to us all: it's incredible how brave you have been this past year, beating cancer. I just wish I'd not been so distracted writing this book, and briefly getting lost again in the chemsex world, and that I had been there for you when you needed me the most. But, my God, you've set a great example for me to follow: I really admire your courage. And I love my stepdad, Phil, for being that rock you needed as you fought your battle.

The last person I must acknowledge is someone central to chemsex culture, not just in London, but who is now a global influence. It's not somebody distributing drugs; it is someone who provides lifesaving support, signposting the avenues that lead out of the culture, and giving expert advice that enables those trapped by chemsex to make the changes they need to make to get their lives back on track. I'm talking, of course, about David Stuart. David, what you do is beyond comprehension. I'd like to thank you from the bottom of my heart on behalf of everybody you have helped.

ADVICE AND SUPPORT SERVICES

56 Dean Street
www.dean.st

After Party Service
www.afterparty.org.uk

The Albert Kennedy Trust
www.akt.org.uk

Galop
www.Galop.org.uk

LGBT Foundation
www.lgbt.foundation

London Friend
www.londonfriend.org.uk

MEN R US
www.menrus.co.uk

NHS Drug and Alcohol Services
www.nhs.uk/Service-Search/Drug-and-alcohol-Services/LocationSearch/496

The Northern
www.thenorthernsexualhealth.co.uk